THE Lucky GUIDE TO MASTERING ANY STYLE

THE **Lucky** GUIDE TO MASTERING ANY STYLE

KIM FRANCE and ANDREA LINETT

GOTHAM
BOOKS

MELCHER
MEDIA

contents

Introduction by
Kim France and Andrea Linett
page 6

Chapter 1 **euro chic** 8
Chapter 2 **california casual** 36
Chapter 3 **rock and roll** 64
Chapter 4 **posh eclectic** 92
Chapter 5 **mod** 118
Chapter 6 **american classic** 146
Chapter 7 **bombshell** 178

Chapter 8 **arty slick** 210

Chapter 9 **bohemian** 236

Chapter 10 **gamine**...............................264

Chapter 11 **mix and match** 292

Lucky Breaks: Exclusive Deals,
Discounts & Giveaways 300

Designer Credits...308

Photography Credits and Acknowledgments 310

Practically everyone at *Lucky* has an inspiration board of some sort, the same tacked-to-the-wall scramble of photographs we hung in our rooms as teenagers and that, today, we see lining the studios of our favorite designers. The images—of certain women at particular, quintessentially stylish moments in their lives—reappear, inspiring reinterpretation, again and again, decade after decade, everywhere from the runway to the street.

These are the styles we always return to, regardless of the trend of the moment; the iconic looks that stick in our consciousness and influence the way we dress, every day. When we sat down to write this book, we thought about what made such looks so powerful and realized that for many of them, it was the women attached. How would Jane Birkin wear this trench, versus, say, Audrey Hepburn? Should I go Patti Smith with this white button-down, or Lauren Hutton? This is how all of us and maybe a lot of you, without even realizing it, think about style.

And because we're *Lucky*, we're also very inspired by the women in our midst—who we see in a restaurant or on the street or at a party—who've got it so exactly right that we wish we could figure out some un-stalker-ish way to ask if we could follow them home and view the contents of their closets.

And as it turns out, because we're *Lucky*, we very often go right ahead and risk coming off like stalkers so we can photograph them for the magazine—or, in this case, the book you hold in your hands. The 22 women we have profiled in these pages were chosen for their unique abilities to spin these all-time iconic looks into something of-the-moment and uniquely their own. We invited them into the studio, and they arrived with literally suitcases full of their own stuff. The voyeuristic thrill of having someone dump out the contents of her closet and explain it to you, piece by piece, is not to be underestimated; seeing real collections instead of fashion collections gives you a new perspective on how style comes about.

Here's what we'd like you to remember as you go through these pages: Like every issue of *Lucky*, this is a guide and not a series of dictates. It's something to have in your head when you're deciding how to put everything together. Know that as we composed each chapter, we were careful to create versions of each look that felt achievable in real life as opposed to possibly-a-bit-too-literal and therefore costumey (hence, no white go-go boots in the Mod chapter.)

Finally, don't be afraid to bend every rule we've laid down here. Use this guide for inspiration (and feel free to mix looks up: see page 292). Most of all, have fun with it. We had a lot of fun making it for you.

—Kim France and Andrea Linett

euro chic

These are the women for whom the word "chic" was invented, though by now that word hardly seems to do them justice. The ones who—at the collections—make all of the fashion editors take notice and bow to perfection. There's a sense of selectiveness and couture to everything they wear—expensive or not—and to how they wear it, as well. In sweaters of the thinnest cashmere and crocodile heels, Catherine Deneuve is the most classic and enduring iteration of the look. But its modern evolution is illustrated best by French *Vogue* fashion director, Emmanuelle Alt, who brilliantly combines pieces like leggings and oversize tees with high-fashion, dramatic items in a way that's as edgy as it is elegant. "The thing that is different about European chic is that it is effortless and sophisticated," says designer Diane von Furstenberg. "The important part is the eclectic part—not what you wear, what you punctuate things with."

This page: Bianca Jagger, 1976. Opposite page, clockwise from top left: Charlotte Rampling, 1982; Marisa Berenson, 1969; Catherine Deneuve, 1965; Emmanuelle Alt, 2007; Inès de la Fressange, 2005; Princess Caroline of Monaco, 1985.

euro chic
essential pieces

silk tie-neck blouse

tailored ruffled button-down

sheer lace blouse

silk shirtdress

skinny knit dress

cap-sleeved shift

camel cashmere overcoat

jewel-tone winter coat

elegant wrap coat

dramatic cocktail dress

sexy multilayered
chiffon dress

day shift with pintuck
detail

euro chic
essential pieces

satin-trim tuxedo jacket

super-snug peplum jacket

contrast-trim cardigan

narrow-fit satin pants

flat-front work pants

fitted white trousers

silk and lace lingerie top

sequined tank

plunging tie-front blouse

shawl-collar jacket

classic bouclé jacket

collarless wool jacket

draped ruched pencil skirt

pleated taffeta skirt

poufy party skirt

euro chic
essential accessories

quilted leather bag

structured day bag

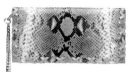

snakeskin clutch

cashmere and leather
gloves

luxe weekend duffel

skinny black belt

leather and
chain-link belt

hefty gold ring

hinged gold bangle

gold and onyx bracelet

fancy everyday watch

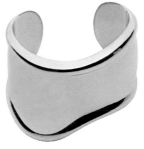

sculptural gold cuff

snakeskin bangles

crocodile t-straps

high-heeled oxfords

woven heels

peep-toe platform
slingbacks

black leather ankle boots

euro chic
how to get the look

FIT AND STYLING:
The Perfect Oversize Blazer

This is the kind of piece that defines the modern-day Euro Chic girl. It's recognizable by its just-right length and beautifully tailored fit. Though the idea is "I'm wearing a menswear blazer," the look couldn't be sexier, especially paired with black leggings and heels. Look for one with the following details:

- The shoulder should fit snugly, without any slouch. "Oversize" here is all about length, not width.

- Shades of gray, black, or navy.

- Slim lapels and two or three buttons on the front.

KEY ACCESSORY:
The Statement Watch

A chunky, glamorous-looking watch instantly conveys style and substance. It doesn't need to be expensive; it just has to have that rich, diver's watch look about it—silver or gold finish, a simple white or black face, and few extra embellishments.

The Endlessly Versatile Big Scarf

This is what separates the women from the girls—the ability to fold, knot, sling, sash, or loop a big scarf. For starters, choose a generous, versatile size, like 28" x 28", so you can wear it a bunch of different ways—knotted around your shoulders, or folded and wrapped around your neck. No matter what, a big scarf is womanly and dramatic; a subtle logo looks chic, but solid colors, soft florals, or funky graphics work equally as well.

Euro Chic Jeans

There's something so best-of-both-worlds about jeans that are tailored like wide, cuffed trousers. The cut should be fitted in the rear, a little higher on the waist, and long enough to sweep (but not puddle on) the ground. Choose a pair in dark, stiff denim. They're retro-cute with canvas sneakers or sophisticated with killer heels or platforms.

how to get the look

THE ESSENTIAL:
Elegant Day Dress

This dress is just so perfectly simple. Take your cues from the icons here—Catherine Deneuve in *Belle de Jour*—classic, lady-like, and totally posh. The fit should be immaculate, with the hem hitting anywhere from just above to just below the knee. Soft tailored details, like a ruffled neckline, contrasting cuffs, collars and buttons, and pretty pintucks add to the overall look. Pair it with some gorgeous patent leather heels and a good handbag, and you're best-dressed material.

Smarten Up with a Jacket-Style Cardigan

The contrast-trim cardigan is especially effective for dressing up jeans. Wear it over a white tank top with dark denim—the result is elegant and rich-looking. If you wear it with skirts, it can look too prim, so make sure you wear your sexiest, least sensible shoes.

ICONIC ITEM:
The Silk Blouse

This polished and incredibly feminine blouse works wonders glamming up day pieces, so it shouldn't be sheer, just thin and delicate-looking. It looks best in shades of black, cream, or deep red. Skip glossy satin silks and opt for washed matte ones—they're more sophisticated.

euro chic
Lucky Girl
Jennifer Alfano

OCCUPATION: Bag Designer
LOCATION: Bronxville, NY

A former fashion editor, Jennifer Alfano started her line of bags in 2006 after years of frustration trying to find one that was exactly what she herself was looking for: not too showy, but not too plain, the one that looked somehow just…right. In short, she says, "I don't want a bag that speaks louder than the person holding it."

This is a pretty dead-on description of Alfano's signature uptown-downtown, minimal-but-not-too-much-so glamour. "I like getting dressed up in feminine things like high heels and pencil skirts, but I don't like 'fussy,'" she says. Alfano gravitates toward more classic pieces with interesting twists to them—a Balenciaga riding jacket that's cut extra long in the back, or a black Rochas skirt suit made entirely of lace. The key to everything, she says, is the right jacket: "They direct the mood of an outfit. They do all the work for you in terms of looking good."

Her closet, which expertly balances high-end designers with an equal dose of more inexpensive names like Banana Republic, is true to her sense of self. "I know my style by now," she says. "I can look at something and say, 'So cute, but not for me.'"

Jennifer's Favorites

Stores: Jeffrey (they have amazing shoes); Dighton Rhode in Greenwich, CT (for designers like Lanvin and Sari Gueron); J.Crew (for basics, summer skirts, and cashmere sweaters); Vince (for simple dresses)

Online store: net-a-porter.com

Style era: Europe in the '60s

Style icons: Monica Vitti, Lee Radziwill, and Ali MacGraw

Colors to wear: Gray, navy, and taupe

Movies that inspire my style: I love old Italian movies from the '60s—*L'Avventura, La Dolce Vita, 8½.*

From Jennifer's Closet

1.
Prada trench
There is something *très français* and *mystérieux* about a trench. Plus, you just look instantly pulled together. I wear this one with dresses and heels or capris and ballet flats.

2.
Jennifer Alfano natural python handbag
The Karina shoulder bag is my answer to a ladies-who-lunch day bag. I like to think it is a bit cooler, and I can't resist the clink of a hardware chain.

3.
Balenciaga wide black belt
This was a splurge—I didn't think I would wear it, but I do. I like it with simple dresses or pencil skirts and blouses. It adds an elegant polish to almost anything.

4.
Balenciaga bronze peep-toe strappy heeled sandals
I love a serious, not prissy, heel. And metallic is surprisingly versatile—it goes with taupe, black, violet, even with my striped sweater and jeans.

5.
Balenciaga navy-and-white striped sweater

This is a sophisticated twist on another classic. I adore the crazy emblem on it, and the sleeves are extra long and skinny, which gives this piece an edge.

6.
Cartier watch

I like a big, clunky, glamorous watch. I have a stainless steel Rolex for winter, and this gold Cartier for the summer.

7.
Derek Lam white short-sleeved jacket

This linen jacket is a staple in the spring and summer—whether I use it to dress up a tank top and jeans or wear it over a sundress for work.

8.
Jennifer Alfano Getaway bag in amethyst python

I wanted to create an oversize but not sloppy everyday tote. This bag is named after *The Getaway*, which stars Ali MacGraw, one of my favorite style icons. She got the European/American thing so right.

9.
Gold chain-link bracelet

When I was a teenager, I was kind of punk—I wore pointy shoes and an armful of bracelets; this bracelet is a nod to that aesthetic, but in a clean, grown-up way.

"I don't like dainty things. All of my jewelry is **REALLY CHUNKY.** I have a lot of vintage '60s and '70s pieces, like big cocktail rings."

putting it together

A classic bouclé jacket with a ruched pencil skirt is a spot-on uptown-downtown combination.

Strappy gold sandals glam up a tie-neck blouse and flat-front black pants for nighttime.

A multilayered chiffon dress with peep-toe heels is elegant evening worthy.

Make a poufy party skirt funky with a sequined tank top and chunky heels.

Elevate a khaki pencil skirt and white ruffled blouse with glossy round-toe heels.

Accent a tie-front blouse and satin pants with logo flats in a high-impact cherry red.

euro chic
all year long

ladylike
jacket

winter

Channel Italian-film-star glamour by adding a scarf-neck sweater, wide-leg trousers, and patent leather heels.

spring

The jacket is just right for the fresh weather balanced with an eyelet tunic, slim black pants, and not-too-fussy (but definitely sexy) heels.

summer

Over drapey but well-cut separates and elegant silver flats, the jacket is sophisticated enough to go from day to dinner.

fall

For a fancy cocktail party, it's that covered-up-yet-suggestive final touch to a provocative dress and sexy accessories.

euro chic
Lucky Girl
Kate Wright

OCCUPATION: Co-owner, Moka
LOCATION: Windsor, CA

Kate Wright, co-owner and buyer for the high-end Windsor, California, boutique Moka, puts a premium on looking pulled together every day, and she's gotten quite good at it. "Basically, I stick to items with clean lines that are easy to wear," she says. "And, I must admit, I buy almost everything in black—that makes getting dressed a lot easier."

With a shop full of big-name labels—Zac Posen, Marc Jacobs, Narciso Rodriguez—at her disposal, she dresses on the higher end of the fashion food chain, but always with restraint. Wright likes to keep her silhouette narrow and fitted—no slouchy sweaters or baggy pants—and her daily uniform is as basic as it gets: For summer, she likes pencil skirts and short-sleeved blouses; for winter, skinny jeans, fitted white tees, and an oversize tailored blazer.

Wright has two essentials no matter what the day: "I never leave the house without an Hermès scarf tied on in some way and a pair of really beautiful high heels," she says. And she does mean always. "Peep-toe pumps, knee-high boots, slingbacks—I'm obsessed."

Kate's Favorites

Stores: Barneys New York; Uniqlo (for fabulous, cheap cashmere); Bergdorf Goodman (for shoes)

Online stores: yoox.com, neimanmarcus.com

Style era: The Edwardian era, 1901–1910, because it marked the start of the dress reform era, when the stiff formality in dressing gave way to a sense of sleek, casual style

Style icon: Coco Chanel. I find her so amazing and ahead of her time: her vision, her grace, her perseverance.

What I listen to while getting ready for a night out: The Killers and my long-standing favorite, U2

What's worth the investment: Anything Chanel, anything Zac Posen, Barbara Bixby Keys of Life necklaces, and Hermès bracelets

I can't live without: An Hermès scarf

Signature scent: Ananas Fizz by L'Artisan Parfumeur

From Kate's Closet

1.
Nicole Farhi black double-breasted trench

I wear this with a black belt cinched at the waist. Not only does the trench make my outfit, it sometimes *is* the outfit when I just want to wear comfortable leggings with it.

2.
Zac Posen gold sleeveless top

This looks great paired with a pencil skirt. It's not too heavy on the gold, and I can dress it up or down.

3.
Hermès bracelets

I can't leave the house without some of these bangles stacked together. I pair them with everything just to add a little something extra.

4.
Brown leather heeled boots with gold hardware

I special-ordered these from Georgina Goodman. I like to wear them with black tights and a Vince dress. It's my no-fuss uniform.

5.
Yves Saint Laurent black leather bag

This is my everyday bag. It holds a ton and doesn't show the wear.

6.
Yigal Azrouël brown pinstriped vest

This vest is perfect for me. I wear it with a fitted white-collared blouse and skinny black jeans.

7.
Manolo Blahnik python pumps

I wear them mostly with jeans because the python is a nice alternative to just wearing black.

8.
Lenny bikini

I don't go on vacation without my Lenny swimsuit. I think they make the most flattering and comfortable swimwear on the market. When I wear this, I always feel like I have the most unique suit on.

9.
David Yurman silver ring with black stone

This is one of my favorite rings. I love the chunkiness of it.

10.
Lenny sheer, sleeveless, deep V-neck dress

This is such a versatile piece. It comes with a slip, so I can wear it out on a hot day as a dress or just use it as a cover-up.

"I have two little kids, and there was a period when I stayed home and took care of them and didn't get dressed up. When I decided to open my store, I definitely made the decision to make myself **MORE SOPHISTICATED.**"

Business Meeting
wrap sweater + **pinstriped trousers** + t-strap pumps

Cocktail Party
chiffon trapeze top + **pinstriped trousers** + gold heels

smart shopping

Get the right silhouette

When choosing a shirt to tuck into skirts and pants, look for a thin fabric and make sure it's not so loosely cut that the excess fabric gathers up and blouses out awkwardly. Tuck the tails of your shirt into your underwear or stockings if possible, and check that there's no tell-tale bulge visible.

Know your faux

In a dream world, we'd all be able to do like Deneuve and buy ourselves a crocodile bag, but obviously that's not an option for many of us. Happily, there are plenty of well-priced bags made out of textured leather— whether mock-crocodile, snakeskin, or ostrich—that are dead ringers for the real thing.

Wear unexpected accessories

There's a fine line between looking refined and looking age-inappropriate— especially when it comes to the grande-dame flourishes (pearls, gold jewelry, ladylike bags) that define this look. If you feel uncomfortable wearing the classics, look for more modern spins on them: timeless jewelry that's a little different, like gray pearls or yellow diamonds and traditional-shaped bags in unexpected hues like sky blue or green.

Where to buy a statement watch

Shocking but true: You can find a chunky, glamorous-looking watch anywhere—even at the drugstore. Keep your eye out for a big, metal link menswear style. If it's so big it slips off your wrist, take it to a jeweler and have a few links removed.

euro chic
store guide

Bergdorf Goodman:
This storied New York behemoth oozes sophistication, housing an unparalleled range of high-end ladylike clothing from Chanel, Carolina Herrera, Fendi, and Michael Kors—with younger lines like Tuleh and Narciso Rodriguez rounding out the mix. **New York, NY, 800-558-1855, bergdorfgoodman.com**

Belgian Shoes: Topped with a signature bow, the ladylike "Belgian" slippers that this Manhattan store—founded by famed retailer Henri Bendel in 1956—is known for have a serious following among a certain subsection of the Upper East Side. Soft soled and available in every conceivable color and fabric iteration (from linen to leather, bright tangerine to muted lavender), the structured, old-fashioned shoes are available online too. **New York, NY, 212-755-7372, belgianshoes.com**

Cartier: This French institution's infinitely appealing Tank watch is a signature wear-it-every-day part of the Euro Chic uniform—as appropriate on a 25-year-old as it is on her grandmother. We're also enchanted by the Love bangles and tricolor rolling rings. **cartier.com for locations**

Chuckies: Don't let the silly name throw you off: Serious uptown ladies flock to this chandelier-lit, boudoir-like shoe salon for its exceptionally deep selection of heels from Jimmy Choo, Prada, and Gucci. **New York, NY, 877-693-9898, chuckiesnewyork.com**

Reiss: One of *Lucky*'s new favorite imports, this British high-street chain specializes in clothes with the kind of sophisticated shapes and vintage details that make it hard to believe they're mass-produced. Look for flatteringly feminine dresses and pintucked blouses. **reiss.co.uk for locations**

Club Monaco: Clean, spare, and modern, outposts of this much-loved line have the feel of a well-edited walk-in closet. The icily cool palette—balanced by carefully chosen shots of bright color—turns up on work clothes as well as partywear. The silhouettes are cut longer and leaner than other big chains, which transform even the humblest of tank tops into something supremely elegant. **clubmonaco.com for locations**

Hermès: If this category had to reduce its essence to a single icon, it would be a simple line drawing of the esteemed Birkin bag, but for hardcore Hermès fans, New York's Madison Avenue store provides endless inspiration. A certain brand of Hermès obsessive heads straight to scarves; another goes hypnotic while staring at the highly detailed, colorful enamel bracelets; others head straight for the watches. The leather cuffs and bracelets attract a younger clientele and can be had at (relatively) reasonable prices. **hermes.com for locations**

Tomas Maier: Even if you're armed with directions, this multi-room bungalow—hidden behind a giant hedge—is tough to find. It's well worth the search, though, because Tomas Maier, who is also creative director of venerable Italian design house Bottega Veneta, stocks the place with impossible-to-find bags from the collection, tribal jewelry, his own line of swimsuits, and impeccably cut sweaters, plus picks from Marni and Azzedine Alaïa. **Miami, FL, 888-373-0707, tomasmaier.com**

Decades: There's vintage shopping, and then there's true vintage shopping, and Decades traffics in the latter, offering extremely rare pieces from high points in the history of various fashion houses. You'll find Yves Saint Laurent from the designer's golden era, a huge selection of vintage Hermès Birkins, and form-fitting long jersey dresses from Azzaro. **Los Angeles, CA, 323-655-0223, decadesinc.com**

california casual

This is a look that is grounded in a time

and place that may never have existed outside of our collective imagination: the tawny, golden-edged Malibu of the '70s—possibly embodied by Farrah Fawcett in a white halter dress at sunset, glass of wine in hand. As John Phillips of the '60s group The Mamas & the Papas put it when he first spied his future wife—and the quintessential California girl—Michelle Phillips, "She stepped out of a dream." And it is the combination of this dreamy sexuality and surfer-girl vitality that makes this look so distinct— and distinctly American. Glamour is in the details here, but on first inspection one might not detect it: It's in a vintagey silk dress that drapes exactly right; a thin, clean, well-cut cotton tee; a delicate gold ring. If ever there were a style of dress for which the word "breezy" applied, this is it: Even at their fanciest, these are clothes that would be right at home at a beach bonfire.

This page: Goldie Hawn, 1992. Opposite page, clockwise from top left: Julie Christie, date unknown; Farrah Fawcett, 1975; Joni Mitchell, 1960; Cameron Diaz, 2003; Michelle Phillips, 1970.

california casual
essential pieces

vintagey scarf blouse

floral wrap blouse

hooded windbreaker

skinny khaki pants

dark stretch jeans

faded drawstring jeans

bandeau bikini   string bikini   white halter vest

lightweight suede skirt   a-line wrap skirt   handkerchief-hem skirt

denim pencil skirt   denim cutoffs   corduroy miniskirt

california casual
essential pieces

heather gray
crewneck t-shirt

colorful scoopneck t-shirt

spaghetti-strap tank

plaid shirt

flutter-sleeved tunic

brown suede poncho

crinkled silk halter dress

bright evening dress

obi-belt slipdress

belted jersey wrap dress

strapless floral sundress

empire-waist dress

california casual
essential accessories

Birkenstock sandals

stack-heeled ankle boots

slouchy leather carryall

high-heeled sandals

gladiator sandals

sporty striped belt

low-key
evening clutch

vintagey drawstring satchel

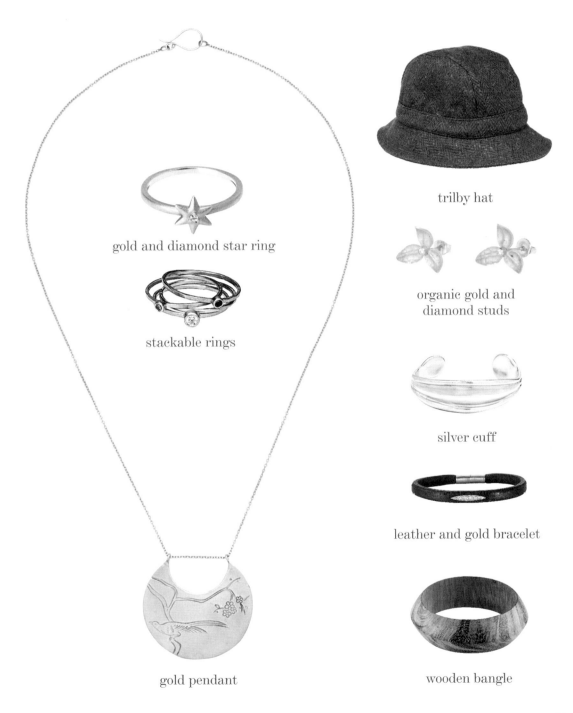

gold and diamond star ring

stackable rings

gold pendant

trilby hat

organic gold and
diamond studs

silver cuff

leather and gold bracelet

wooden bangle

how to get the look

FIT AND STYLING:
The Perfect Tank

This is a more refined piece than at first it may appear. The feel and fine-tuned details are really important to get right, so look for these elements:

• **A longer length with a hem** that hits past the hips or even the top of the thighs, so it looks almost like a dress that's been cut to tunic length.

• **Thin or spaghetti straps,** which are more sexy than sporty.

• **White, black, and solid** colors—they just look more grown-up than patterns.

Choose the Right-Length Miniskirt

The California Casual mini is not about being crazy-sexy-hot. At all. It's loose, lower-slung, and all about being comfortable. Choose one with a mid-thigh or longer length (whatever suits your figure best) and a waistline that sits right on your hip. In terms of shape, the best ones flare out a touch rather than jut down straight. We love it in corduroy, which is so old-school surfer chick. This is a daytime piece so pair it with basic T-shirts or beachy sandals rather than trying to dress it up for night.

All About Drawstring Pants

The type of material determines when and where to wear drawstring pants. Silk, satin, and linen are elegant for evening—they look great with a simple silk camisole in a similar, but not matching, shade, like cream with white, soft black with indigo, dark gray with light gray. Add big gold hoops, some bangles, and flat sandals, and you're set. Cotton and canvas pants are strictly for playtime.

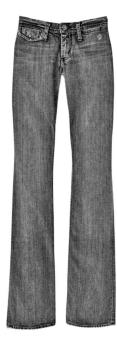

California Casual Jeans

These should fit well in the rear, but be relaxed throughout the leg: not so wide that you can't see where your knees are, but not so skinny that you can't bounce around on the beach. What makes these so appealingly vintagey is a mid-rise waist and a faded, soft denim that looks like it's been washed a million times.

Try a Western-Style Plaid Button-Down

Though it may not be obvious, the western-style plaid shirt is *very* California Casual. It's a natural with jeans and shorts, but don't be afraid to be subversive and make a little statement by tucking it into an elegant, high-waisted skirt for a funky, laid-back kind of glamour. Big pockets look authentically western, and if the fit is skinny and the fabric thin, it's a truly foolproof piece.

how to get the look

The Versatile Jersey Dress

Casual enough for running errands, this drapey tank-top dress can be any length from knee to floor. Once again, the fit is body-skimming, but not so tight that it shows if you just ate lunch. A belted waist looks cute and drapes nicely too. If you can get away without wearing a bra, skip it, but if you can't, throw a tank top on underneath so that the bra straps don't show.

KEY ACCESSORY:
Aviators

Aviators never look dated, and if you can pull them off—they don't work for every face shape—they're really sexy. We like to stick with the classics here: brown or green lenses and a bronzy frame.

The Denim Cutoffs

These are not Daisy Dukes. The inseam should be about three
inches from the crotch to the hem, which is surfer-style and totally
flattering. The hips and thigh should be fitted along the lines of
the leg. The waist should be low, but not hip-bone low.

MUST-HAVE SHOE:
Gladiator Sandals

These sandals are a simple touch that sets the mood. Look for ones
with feminine, narrow leather bands, and play around with how you
pair them for the best look on you—some people can pull them off
with short hemlines, but most of us can't. Try them with long, flowy
sundresses or cropped jeans instead.

47

california casual
Lucky Girl
Rashida Jones

OCCUPATION: Actress
LOCATION: Los Angeles, CA

"I've pretty much always been bicoastal between New York and L.A., and my style reflects that," says actress Rashida Jones, whose look is a clean fusion of bright, '70s-inpired casual—soft cotton T-shirts, frayed miniskirts, and paper-thin gold jewelry—and classic East Coast minimalism. "I like to put a structured blazer over a T-shirt with shorts, or a sweater vest over a sundress. I want everything I wear to be a tailored version of casual." Likewise, she is inspired by her memories of how California women dressed when she was a child. "They were so feminine and chic," she says. "Things were so simple and drapey, meant to show off a woman's shape."

Her mixture of breezy and sleek begins and ends with a great white T-shirt and a pair of sexy but comfortable shoes: "I don't think shoes have to be pointy and high to be glamorous." Her favorites "are a pair of Repetto sandals that are basically a sole, a tiny piece of thin suede, and a little elastic around the foot. They're so sexy."

Her biggest rule, she says, is to dress for your body type. "I know boot-cut jeans look best on me, even if they're not 'of the season,' so that's what I keep on wearing."

Rashida's Favorites

Stores: I love Steven Alan and Hillary Rush for all my basics, and Curve and Diavolina for beautiful party pieces. And H&M is just a brilliant thing.
Online store: net-a-porter.com, yoox.com, eBay, jcrew.com
Style icons: Jane Birkin, Audrey Hepburn, and Jean Shrimpton
Colors: I'm a big fan of black and navy, fuchsia and kelly green.
Movies that inspire my style: *Network*, *Rushmore*, *Nine to Five*
What I listen to while getting ready for a night out: Kanye West and Jay-Z. But I have to be careful because if I get too into it, the party might just have to stay at home. It's happened before.
I can't live without: A perfect white tank top
Signature scent: Midnight Orchid by Susanne Lang

From Rashida's Closet

1.
Moschino sleeveless black cotton top
I love the original detailing on this—it's basic but really pretty.

2.
Repetto black leather ballet flats
Even though I'm short, I love my flats. I have ballet flats in all kinds of colors and fabrics.

3.
R&Y Augousti black leather shoulder bag
I keep getting the same kind of handbag over and over again—I love the soft black leather. I carry this from day to night, so I like to invest in something I really like.

4.
Steven Alan purple-and-white gingham button-front shirt
Steven Alan button-downs are perfect—they always look good no matter where you are or what else you have on.

5.
Gold hoop earrings
I like how delicate and slim
these are.

6.
Gerard Darel cream blazer
This blazer is brilliantly constructed—
it's so flattering on.

7.
J Brand deep indigo
straight-leg denim jeans
I love the dark, but not
oversaturated, hue and the
super-flattering cut.

"I like dresses that are very simple, but have some original detail, like **A BIT OF RUCHING** along the neckline. I don't think something needs to be outrageous to be chic."

california casual
putting it together

Drawstring jeans paired with a windbreaker and Birkenstocks are chic in a surfer-casual way.

Denim cutoffs and a wrap blouse complement sandals and an oversize carryall.

A crinkled silk halter dress is both easy to wear and elegant with wedges and a clutch.

Bring understated glamour to a bright evening dress with metallic sandals.

A scarf blouse adds a vintagey element to crisp skinny khaki pants and retro wedges.

A strapless sundress is comfortable and feminine with sandals and a drawstring satchel.

**slouchy
knit top**

winter

The thin texture and extra length make the top just right with a moody, night-out ensemble of a bomber jacket, dark denim, and fold-over boots.

spring

For the right blend of earthy and polished, use the top in place of a T-shirt with a denim vest, short shorts, and sandals.

summer

Throw it on over a bikini, along with sexy sandals and a straw bag to look effortlessly glamorous at the beach.

fall

As a drapey base for spiffy office separates, it keeps the mood loosely feminine without looking sloppy.

california casual
Lucky Girl
Charlotte Ronson

OCCUPATION: Clothing Designer
LOCATION: New York, NY

Charlotte Ronson—all long legs, tawny skin, and streaky blond hair—looks like she was born to be barefoot. That innate ease is coupled with an equally easy sense of style, which pretty much explains the appeal of the clothes she designs as well: pieces that are young, unpretentious, and above all else, cool without trying too hard—just like Ronson herself.

Often found in jeans, a super-thin vintage T-shirt, and an ocean blue pedicure, Ronson clearly knows her milieu. "I love anything crocheted and anything neon pink," she says. She has an eclectic array of jewelry—feather-motif silver earrings, colorful string bracelets—but only chooses pieces that are lightweight and finespun, so that she can pile on as little or as much as she likes without fear of looking overdone. "Everything I wear has to be something I can just throw on and walk out the door in. The only time you'll see me really dressed up is if I'm a bridesmaid at a wedding."

Charlotte's Favorites

Stores: Opening Ceremony; Eden Manor; Ella May and Alternative Apparel (for tees); Mayle (for accessories); Steven Alan; I Heart
Style icons: Audrey Hepburn, Brigitte Bardot, and Kate Moss
Movies that inspire my style: *Kansas City Bomber* and *Bugsy Malone*. In *Bugsy Malone*, Jodie Foster played the character Tallulah, the nightclub singer. I loved everything about her, from her name to the way she dressed, talked, and sang. She was amazing.
What I listen to while getting ready for a night out: The Black Crowes' *Amorica*; The Beatles' *Revolver*; Amy Winehouse's *Back to Black*; Regina Spektor's *Begin to Hope*; Joni Mitchell's *Blue*; Cat Stevens' *Greatest Hits*; Johnny Cash's *American IV: The Man Comes Around*; Mark Ronson's *Version*
Vacation spot: Harbour Island in the Bahamas

From Charlotte's Closet

1.
Charlotte Ronson
striped tunic

This is really cute with little shorts or a skirt. I like the oatmeal and gray shades—they make it look softer and washed out.

2.
Ray-Ban sunglasses

I'm a big fan of classic Ray-Bans. They're smaller, so they fit my face better than other sunglasses.

3.
Charlotte Ronson
board shorts

I designed these to be like old-school surfer shorts, but cut for a girl. They're not too short or too long, and I love the way they look in white corduroy.

4.
Charlotte Ronson
short-sleeved knit dress

So summery and vintage. I love anything crocheted and '70s-style. It just reminds me of summer.

"I like to experiment with **COLOR AND PATTERNS**—but certain things about my style never change. I never wear long skirts or anything that's too fancy or looks too new."

5.
Balenciaga lizard heels
I bought these at Satine in L.A. I like that they're green but still very classic and ladylike.

6.
Black bikini with pink flowers
The print on this bikini is really fun. It has touches of fluorescent pink, which I'm a sucker for.

7.
Shell ring with purple stone
The models wore these rings during one of my fashion shows. I liked it so much I also got one for my mom in a silver-gray stone. It's a bit bigger than mine.

8.
Gold shark-tooth necklace
I found this when I was looking for a present for my friend. I ended up buying it for myself and giving her a different one.

9.
Wish bracelet
I've had this since I was a little girl. I bought it from a woman on the beach in Ibiza. They come in many colors, and each color means something different.

Dinner Party

dolman-sleeved top + **boot-cut jeans** + strappy sandals

Beach Date

vintage camisole + **boot-cut jeans** + suede sandals

60

smart shopping

Pick the right jersey material

Always look for smooth-cotton jersey dresses that are prewashed, since jersey tends to shrink. Matte jersey (which has silk crepe in the blend and is a finer material than traditional jersey) and washed silks are good alternatives—drapey and loose, but still elegant. Heavy-textured jersey can add bulk, while material that is too skinny-silky can reveal every lump and bump.

Pay special attention to wrap skirts

These can be deceptive in their coverage, so make sure there's enough fabric to cover you when you're walking and that it's not constantly unwrapping and exposing your legs. These skirts are often made of sheer material, so see how it looks in different mirrors and under different lights.

Shop department stores

For sophisticated nighttime tees, look in the lingerie section of a department store—the ones you'll find there will have delicate, simple cuts and are of reliably great quality.

Buy bikinis carefully

If you're buying a bikini online, your best chance for the right fit is with a string bikini. Because both the top and bottom have adjustable ties, they can easily conform to your figure. (And this style is surprisingly flattering to a variety of body types—trust us.)

Make your own jewelry

Rather than buying an expensive, long beaded necklace at a boutique—you'd be amazed at the markup—string your own at a bead store. It's fun and practical.

Foley + Corinna:

Occupying baroque-inspired spaces—complete with velveteen furnishings and ornate wallpaper—on both coasts, owners Dana Foley and Anna Corinna are devoted to a gypsy-luxe aesthetic. Both spots blend Foley's signature draped jersey pieces with Corinna's impeccably sourced vintage clothing and collection of slouchy bags crafted from the softest leathers. **New York, NY, 212-529-2338, and Los Angeles, CA, 323-944-0169, foleyandcorinna.com**

Calypso:

With an outpost in almost every beach-centric locale in the world, from the Hamptons to Saint-Tropez, this Saint Barth's–based chainlet specializes in reliably effortless vacation wear, like long raw-silk party dresses, loose-knit sweaters, and metallic sandals. **calypso-celle.com for locations**

Fred Segal:

The Melrose branch of this legendary L.A. retailer is where stars and hipsters stock up on everything from layerable paper-thin tanks by Pete to tie-waisted dresses by Tucker. Plus, it arguably has one of the more comprehensive jeans selections in the city. **Los Angeles, CA, 310-394-7535, fredsegal.com**

Key:

Airy and skylit, this spot has the feel of an artist's studio. Helmed by two fashion veterans, the store emphasizes subtly glamorous picks from emerging designers: Long jersey gowns with palm prints from Riller & Fount, pinafore dresses from Anlo Denim, and slinky Yumi Kim tops are all part of the mix. **New York, NY, 212-334-5707, shopkeynyc.com**

Lisa Kline:

Blessed with an insatiable celebrity clientele and a glut of quintessentially California-laid-back labels like Rachel Pally and Madison Marcus, this Hollywood shop is packed with the essential West Coast wardrobe-building staples. **Los Angeles, CA, 310-246-0907, lisakline.com**

Hannah Clark: Housed in an old tenement building, Hannah Clark's creations—opal-studded rings and the daintiest pendants cast after sparrows and cherry blossoms—reside next to similarly gorgeous pieces, like Miki Tanaka's hammered gold necklaces. **New York, NY, 212-539-1970, hannah-clark.com**

Shoprobertson.com: Inspired by one of Hollywood's most celeb-trafficked and boutique-laden thoroughfares, the picks on this site are heavily rooted in Los Angeles' more casual trends. There are smocked dresses from Puella, racerback tanks galore, plus terry shorts from T-Bags.

Diani: From the chocolate-colored Vera Wang Lavender Label jersey dresses and tea-stained Hanii Y. blouson lace tops to the beach-cottagey interior, everything here has the quietly distinct elegance one would expect in this most wealthy of resort towns. **Santa Barbara, CA, 877-342-6474, dianiboutique.com**

Kaight: Kitted out with bamboo floors and industrial steel shelves, Kaight's sleek, earth-friendly interior is a perfect match for the understated eco-conscious merchandise. Everything falls under the organic/ethically produced/fair-trade umbrella, from Anna Cohen's coconut-button trenches to Toms canvas slip-ons. **New York, NY, 212-680-5630, kaightshop.com**

rock
and roll

Who among us has not, at least for a moment, wanted to look as cool as Patti Smith on the cover of *Horses,* or Debbie Harry in the old days of Max's Kansas City, or Kate Moss hanging out at an English rock festival? And yet, without the benefit of being an actual rock star, trying to pull off such a thing seems best left to, well, Kate Moss. The essentials of rock style are no big mystery: jeans and leather pants, a boyish biker jacket, some wicked-looking Portobello Road boots. But it's all a matter of combining these with lots of slink and style and balancing the tough with the ethereal, the strict with the sensuous.

This page: Kate Moss, 2006. Opposite page, clockwise from top left: Chrissie Hynde, 1980; Debbie Harry, 1978; Patti Smith, 1978; Bebe Buell, 1970; Marianne Faithfull and Anita Pallenberg, 1967; Nico, 1966.

motorcycle jacket

white tuxedo jacket

side-zip jacket

ankle-buckle corduroys

skinny red jeans

black cigarette jeans

animal-print camisole

loose-fitting metallic tank

tuxedo shirt

zippered black miniskirt

ultra-sexy pencil skirt

stretchy tube skirt

structured cardigan

ragged-hem
scoopneck top

distressed mohair
sweater

rock and roll
essential pieces

stretchy white t-shirt

dandy vest

skinny tailored black vest

velvet trousers

narrow pinstriped pants

cropped leggings

zippered shift

gothic vintage
evening dress

studded black
cocktail dress

biker cardigan

double-breasted
military-style coat

schoolboy blazer

rock and roll
essential accessories

hot pink suede booties

platform ankle boots

gothic evening heels

black Converse high-tops

over-the-knee boots

thin studded belt

plaid doctor's bag

evening clutch

chain-detail purse

fringe scarf

studded link
bracelet

multistrand
choker

bejeweled
cocktail ring

pointy pavé
diamond ring

how to get the look

FIT AND STYLING:
The Perfect Leather Pants

Where would rock and roll be without great leather pants? Here are some tips for getting the look right:

- **Watch the leather-with-** leather factor. These are statement-making enough on their own that you don't need to add on motorcycle boots *and* a belt *and* jacket.

- **Pull the pants up before you** sit down to keep knees from bagging.

- **Pick a drainpipe or straight-** leg cut and make sure they're long enough to go with heels.

- **To keep them clean, just** pull out the lining (which is usually not attached at the hem), hand-wash it with a bit of soap, and let air dry. Keep the leather soft and supple by buffing it with mink oil and a flannel cloth.

MUST-HAVE SHOE:
Ankle Boots

There's something about Rock-and-Roll style that very often puts focus on the ankle. There are pants with buckles at the ankle, leggings and drainpipe jeans that hug the ankle, and possibly coolest of all, ankle boots, which are just so fun and bad-girl tough. Wear them with bright, contrasting tights or incredibly skinny pants, or an evening dress while everyone else is in strappy heels.

Rock-and-Roll Jeans

Industrial faded denim jeans are edgy-looking and unique to rock and roll. The denim should be thin, and the fit lean enough so they look like leggings. The ideal fit is low-waisted and bunched up at the ankle—equally great with ankle boots or pointy stilettos.

Look Sexy in a Poet's Blouse

A top like this is an easy way to add some drama to your wardrobe. Whether you get one that is wonderfully fitted and tight or flimsy and loose, almost like a Victorian undergarment, make sure the ruffles go all the way up and down the front. We also like ruffled bell sleeves that swing and hang down to your fingertips. So Robert Plant.

Get the Stud Effect Without a Single Stud

Studs are a double-edged sword—they're fundamentally punk, yes, but also so iconic that one can feel in costume when wearing them. Still, metal is such a great flourish. (Think about Elvis in his gold lamé jacket, David Bowie in head-to-toe Ziggy Stardust regalia.) So go for a flash: A glinty gold scarf wrapped around your neck says the same thing as a huge, studded leather belt, just in a softer way. Anything with grommets, chain- and zipper-detailing, or metallic thread woven throughout looks the part.

73

how to get the look

The Rock-and-Roll Evening Dress

There's no hard or fast rule when it comes to this. The dress could be asymmetrical and drapey (like you hemmed it yourself with scissors), gothically tailored and Victorian, or scandalously bare, like it's just about to wantonly fall off your shoulders.

The Authentic Concert T-shirt

This is the calling card of Rock-and-Roll style and the easiest way for anyone to capture the look. In the past, you had to scour vintage stores for a good one (and often pay a fortune), but now you can find beautifully worn-in, extra-soft, and vintagey-looking reproduction concert tees. To get that sexy-without-trying effect, pick one that's a bit oversize and super-thin. You want it to look like it was your high school boyfriend's and you stole it and have had for years. Wear it in its most authentic form: with jeans and boots or sneakers.

ICONIC ITEM:
The Black Leather Jacket

A no-muss, no-fuss, straightforward black leather biker jacket is perhaps the most surprisingly versatile rock-and-roll piece ever—the more beat-up looking, the better. It should be fitted at the shoulders and through the arms, with the hem hitting at the hip. It easily goes from day to night, worn over slouchy pants or floral dresses.

rock and roll
Lucky Girl
Monet Mazur

OCCUPATION: Actress
LOCATION: New York, NY

Monet Mazur got a taste for fashion early: "When I was six, I was obsessed with getting a *Desperately Seeking Susan* jacket like Madonna's," says the actress. Since then she's developed a signature style that is an outgrowth of Madonna's sexy-tough Susan character in the 1985 movie: long on old-school rock-star flair done in a decidedly sexy, feminine way. "I'm into the dramatics of things: capes, hats, spiky gold jewelry," she says. Mazur mixes her favorite knee-high purple boots with a classic-looking bag, black leggings, fringy scarves, leather jackets, and other accoutrements. "For night," she says, "I'll grab a thin, fur-felt fedora and shove all my hair under it to go out, even when it's 75 degrees out." But even at her simplest, Mazur stays true to her look—her two absolute essentials are her tight cigarette jeans in dark blue or black and her classic black Converse sneakers. "I've worn them forever—the high-tops and the low-tops! I got them for my husband and my three-year-old. We all walk around the house in them like we're the Ramones."

Monet's Favorites

Stores: Des Kohan, Alms, Coach, Ella Moss, Splendid, Opening Ceremony, Marc Jacobs, Decades, Shareen Vintage

Online stores: I am an eBay addict! But I also love lagarconne.com and jjhatcenter.com for Borsalino hats.

Style era: The '60s

Style icons: Jane Birkin and Serge Gainsbourg

Movies that inspire my style: *Contempt*, *Breathless*, *Ladies and Gentlemen*, *the Fabulous Stains* (Diane Lane is 15 in this movie, and it is the *craziest* styling you've ever seen!)

What I listen to while getting ready for a night out: Babyshambles' *Down in Albion*

What's worth the investment: An Yves Saint Laurent jacket

Signature scent: Coco Mademoiselle by Chanel, always

From Monet's Closet

1.
Vintage knit cape
I got this at Shareen Vintage in downtown L.A. I go there for super-undercover vintage missions.

2.
Repetto black patent and canvas shoes
I'm so into these shoes, I can't tell you. They are timeless, beautifully handmade, and they fit like gloves. I can't stop buying them!

3.
Hermès Medor watch
My husband bought me this when our son was born. I never take it off.

4.
Shana Lee gold pyramid stud earrings

I wear these every day—I love how simple they are and the cool shape.

5.
Coach brown leather bag

People always comment on this bag, even though it's pretty classic.

6.
Express black leather bomber jacket

It took me years to find a bomber jacket this perfect—I'm obsessed with it. And I love that it's from Express.

7.
Minnetonka black suede moccasins

These are so comfy and great for wearing out and about during the day.

"I used to be a lot more experimental and a bit on the outrageous side, but now that I'm older and married with a son, MY TASTE HAS BECOME MORE CLASSIC. I still like wild pieces, like a crazy deconstructed Galliano minidress, but I'll get it in black now, instead of hot pink."

putting it together

It's irreverent to pair a school-boy blazer with sexier pieces like cropped leggings.

A gothic vintage dress looks seductively tough with black platforms and a slick clutch.

The rich metallic tank elevates the comfortable pairing of a tube skirt and flats.

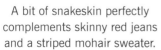

A bit of snakeskin perfectly complements skinny red jeans and a striped mohair sweater.

Ankle-buckle corduroys and a stretchy white T-shirt dress up fast with colorful flats.

There is nothing more Debbie Harry than a zebra print paired with a bright color.

rock and roll
all year long

dandy
suit vest

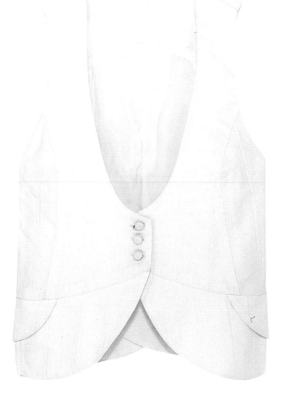

winter

A military jacket, striped sweater, and jeans are a cool combination, but just a little too clean—the vest breaks it all up, lending a bit of spontaneity.

spring

By layering the vest over a floaty dress and finishing the look with suede booties and a hobo, you've got the right blend of moody, pretty, and funky.

summer

Trim pieces with a little edge—a tank top, denim miniskirt, and metallic flats—add up to give a laid-back, chic feel.

fall

The vest acts as the wild-but-not-too-wild factor for an outfit of a ruffle-front blouse, crisp trousers, and a leather jacket.

rock and roll
Lucky Girl
Alexandra Richards

OCCUPATION: Model
LOCATION: New York, NY

Alexandra Richards is the daughter of Keith Richards and Patti Hansen. She comes by her personal style genetically—and she's got a couple of pretty glamorous closets to root around in. "I steal my mom's high heels and my dad's scarves," she says. "He has some from the '60s with skulls all over them, like the Alexander McQueen ones, but original!"

Richards lives in faded black jeans, she loves her leather biker jacket, and she's got the skull rings and aforementioned tatty scarves. And yet she doesn't veer into biker-chick territory; rather, her everyday look is remarkably fresh. "I live in cotton jersey T-shirts, the tissue-thin burnout ones, faded black jeans, and a cool jacket," she says.

Like any good rock-and-roll girl, Richards loves a lot of shine: "I'm obsessed with jewelry," she says. "I have everything—silver bangles and tons of skulls—but I also really like the Diamonds by the Yard from Tiffany's." Her wild/refined mentality applies to nighttime too: During one party-filled week she wore a couture Dior beaded gown one night and denim cutoffs with tights and heels the next.

Alexandra's Favorites

Stores: Ksubi (for jeans); Flying A (for vintage shoes); Poppy on Mott Street (for pretty stuff)
Style icons: My mom and my sister
Movies that inspire my style: *The Darjeeling Limited* or anything by Wes Anderson
What I listen to while getting ready for a night out: Peter Tosh

From Alexandra's Closet

1.
Black graphic tee
My mom wore this when she was pregnant with me and later gave it to me. Now I wear it all the time—it's so easy to throw on.

2.
Skull and cross earrings
I'm an absolute jewelry fiend, but my taste kind of goes to two extremes: I like skulls and diamonds. Usually that means two different looks, but with these, I get the best of both worlds!

3.
Black bustier catsuit
I got this from my mom. It looks super-sexy, but it's also really easy to layer with other things—like a skirt or a big cardigan and my ankle boots, so the effect isn't so *wow*.

4.
Black cardigan
I like that this sweater has a kind of grandpa look, but it's super-thin, not at all bulky, so I can wear it with skinny jeans and not look lopsided. I love boys' cardigans—I steal them from my guy friends.

WILD

5.
Hudson dark indigo skinny jeans

These jeans fit me perfectly. The legs are cut long, which is important if you're tall like I am. I don't have to worry about that "floodwatch" too-short-pant thing happening.

6.
Leopard-print pony-skin heels

I nabbed these from my mom. The heel is not too high, which is good because I can't walk in really high heels. I wear them with everything from dresses to cut-off jean shorts.

7.
Green python bag

When I first saw this bag I went crazy for it. The color is amazing— I like that it's not neutral. It's extra roomy: perfect for when I'm running around town all day long. I can fit a change of clothes in there, no problem.

8.
Brown leather necklace with blue stone pendant

So simple, but so pretty.

9.
Black wool military jacket

This was Anita Pallenberg's from the '60s. It's an authentic military coat, so it's pretty big, but I like to wear it with layers underneath as my winter coat.

"I was a **TOTAL TOMBOY GROWING UP,** and that's still a big part of who I am. But now that I'm older, I appreciate anything by Dolce & Gabbana too."

Club Hopping
leather jacket + **bright red jeans** + ankle booties

Flea Marketing
drapey top + **bright red jeans** + snakeskin flats

smart shopping

Save on accessories

There are plenty of cool-looking, wildly expensive Rock-and-Roll-style accessories out there, but it's so easy (and way more authentic) to buy extras like fringy scarves and silver skull rings from a street vendor or craft fair rather than a fancy boutique.

Copy your favorites

Take a pair of your favorite jeans to your tailor and have them copied in the Rock-and-Roll fabric of your choice—whether it's velveteen, velvet, leather, or super-fine cord.

Buy two pairs

Since ankle boots are so vital to this look, get two pairs if you can—a hip but comfortable pair you can wear for day, and a killer high-heeled pair for night.

Shop chain stores for leather jackets

You don't have to splurge on a leather biker jacket—the rock-and-roll Lucky Girls in this book picked theirs up at chain stores like Express and Top Shop and just broke in the jackets themselves (though a great stylist trick is to weather the leather with sandpaper for a roughened-up, vintagey look that disguises the shiny, plastic-like look of inexpensive leather). What's most important is finding a jacket that's not too loose and not too tight, with minimal bulk—look for a thin lining, flat slash pockets, a simple zipper closure, and either a classic collar or one that zips all the way up your neck.

Trash & Vaudeville:

Salesman Jimmy Webb is enough of an institution to have garnered a 2007 *New Yorker* profile, and at his jam-packed, concert poster–papered East Village landmark—which has graced St. Mark's Place for 30-odd years—he sells everything punk, goth, and in between. From now until forever—or so one hopes—Trash & Vaudeville will be there to dispense skinny leather jeans and Doc Martens to My Chemical Romance, model Agyness Deyn, Avril Lavigne, and suburban wannabes alike. **New York, NY, 212-982-3590**

Apartment: Arguably as famous as Paris' trend-hive Colette and equally exquisitely edited, this dungeon-like space has seriously edgy items you won't find anywhere else. Everything, from spider-festooned bags by Undercover to pleasingly crumpled leather jackets from Rick Owens, subscribes to an am-I-cool-enough-to-pull-this-off sensibility. **Berlin, Germany, 493028042251, apartmentberlin.de**

Bootbarn.com: Best known as a major shopping destination for western footwear, this expansive site also has one of the largest online selections of motorcycle boots, from brands like Harley-Davidson and Frye. Also, for those whose tastes run in a slightly more '80s direction, they've got a major Doc Martens selection.

C'est Magnifique: Since 1959, this old-world, family-owned silversmith has been making jewelry on-site, some of it unbelievably—and delightfully—creepy. We love the dog-skull rings and other gothic curiosities, like pendants in the shape of snakes and arachnids. **New York, NY, 212-475-1613, cest-magnifique.com**

Daryl K: Designer Daryl Kerrigan has been a favorite of just about every cool rock chick—and any-one hoping to inject a dose of rock-chick style into her wardrobe—since she set up shop in the East Village in 1991. Her slick, slightly deconstructed aesthetic is worked into everything from cotton to wool, to weird, space-age materials, and then cut into sophisticated shapes, like button-front minidresses and perfectly cut pants. **New York, NY, 212-529-8790, darylk.com**

Reborn.ws: For the e-commerce extension of her popular Montreal boutique, Brigitte Chartrand, a former stylist, buys in a palette composed almost entirely of black and gray, which keeps the mood of her site impressively edgy—as does the site's fashion-zine design. Chartrand can always be counted on to find the newest of the cool, from forward-thinking designers like Preen, Bless, and Rad Hourani.

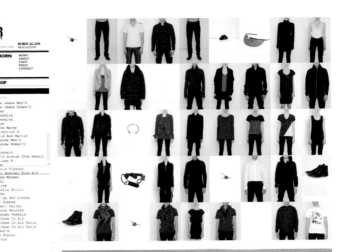

Loveless: This raved-about multilevel shop is exuberantly weird: Its airy upper floors carry more accessible items, like Cacharel dresses, while a baroque-industrial vibe dominates downstairs, from the purposely rust-stained walls and black-crystal chandeliers to the goth- and biker-influenced clothing. **Tokyo, Japan, 81334012301**

Mona Moore: Housed in a gallery-like salon, Mona Moore stocks only the most ferociously hip shapes from designers like Dries Van Noten and Yohji Yamamoto. Owners Anna Maria Varriano and Lisa Bush have—on the strength of their first-rate e-commerce site—earned a huge following in the States as well. Added bonus: Shipping is free to anywhere in North America. **Montreal, Canada, 800-619-0674, monamoore.com**

Very Bad Horse: Steven Tyler has been known to stockpile designer Kim Montenegro's skin-tight jeans, and one only has to try on a pair to understood why: They mold to your body like they're tailor-made, and they instantly endow you with a badass sexiness. **Philadelphia, PA, 215-627-3376, verybadhorse.com**

Wolfgangsvault.com: We're not snobs: Even if you weren't actually there when The Who played Fillmore East in 1968, there's no shame in wearing the (reproduced) concert T-shirt. This site has loads of excellent specimens, all priced for less than $40.

Crazy Pig: Long before rock-and-roll jewelry was part of mainstream cool, Keith Richards and Ozzy Osbourne were turning to this Covent Garden–based store for rings in the shape of skeletal fingers and wolf-head pendants. **London, England, 442072404305, crazypigdesigns.com**

posh
eclectic

"There's a lot more eclecticism and experimentation in Britain than [there is in] French or Italian fashion," says former Chloé designer Phoebe Philo. "Although we're huge snobs, people are into wearing clothes that don't conform." Indeed, when it comes to this category, ordinary conventions of dressing simply do not apply. Instead there's a certain madcap glamour, made up of equal parts country-estate frump and the black-sheep aristocrat's disregard for what's acceptable. But there's a genuine chemistry when it all comes together. To wit: Laura Bailey's loose, fearless layering of decades—'40s librarian with '70s punk with '30s socialite with turn-of-the-century gothic—finished with incredible little couture, vintage-store touches (a sweet cloche hat from the attic, a fur shrug, decadent lace layers).

This page: Helena Christensen, 2004. Opposite page, clockwise from top left: Sophie Dahl, 2006; Laura Bailey, 2003; Jacquetta Wheeler, 2004; Daphne Guinness, 2006; Karen Elson, 2006; Stella Tennant, 2003.

posh eclectic
essential pieces

ruffled houndstooth blazer

lace-cuff edwardian jacket

short-sleeved velvet
day jacket

tapered flat-front
black pants

khaki equestrian pants

cropped trousers

antique lace vest

tiered lace camisole

corsage neckline
chiffon shell

Liberty-print dress

dramatic black
lace wrap

vintagey polka-dot
dress

slim-fit tweed blazer

fair isle cardigan

plaid hunting cape

sheer evening skirt with
velvet detail

button-front
circle skirt

silk velvet
tiered skirt

corset-tailored
cotton blouse

crinkled silk ruffled top

boxy '20s-style blouse

jewel-tone
silk dress

fur-collar
menswear coat

ruffled
double-breasted coat

essential accessories

fabric and rose gold
necklace

antique gold locket

antique watch fob bracelet

embroidered drop earrings

cameo ring

organic pearl ring

tangled chain
and rhinestone choker

multistrand
beaded necklace

lace-up ankle boots

green wellies

sturdy riding boots

peep-toe wedges with
ankle straps

lace-up suede pumps

velvet and gold
t-strap heels

worn-in briefcase bag

canvas and leather
hunting bag

vintage evening bag

how to get the look

Wear an Evening Dress During the Day

Posh Eclectic women are the queens of day-to-night and night-to-day dressing. To them, these are one and the same, and there's no such thing as something too dressy to trot out for lunch. It might be frothy or sequined, or simple and silky—there isn't really a rule here. To wear it for day, mix it in with two (or more, depending on just exactly how eclectic you want to be) pieces that go delightfully against the grain of the dress' fancy mood, like a tweed blazer and sturdy ankle boots, or an oversize sweater and ballet flats. Dark matte tights make a great instant contrast against light floaty styles too.

Hunting for the Perfect Vintage Embellished Sweater

When you want a classic cardigan that's tricked out in some way—whether with beading, a lace collar, or special buttons—the most logical place to look is in vintage stores. Unfortunately, the pieces you find there don't always hold up over time (moth holes, lost beads), so try designers like Rebecca Taylor and Jill Stuart, who can be relied on to turn out stellar versions of these most seasons.

A Contemporary Twist on Riding-Style Trousers

These trousers have that stealthily sexy element—the lean, flat front is very flattering and chic, but because they're sporty, you won't look so much as though you're in tight pants, but rather that you just wandered back from the stables. Key elements to look for are narrow equestrian lines and lots of seams so that they seem like jodhpurs, even if they're not.

Layer with Lace

Using a lace top as a layer instantly adds a level of sultry sophistication to any outfit that might otherwise appear too basic. You can choose a dramatic shape, or layer two pieces without overwhelming the outfit. Lace is fantastic for night, but it also transforms something like jeans and a sweater for day. Don't be afraid to play and pair it with your most workaday pieces.

ICONIC ITEM:
The Wellies

Here's the rule for Wellies: Wear them with a skirt or a mini or jeans or whatever looks cool, but only if the climate is cooperating. If it's not raining and there's no mud, don't push it.

posh eclectic
Lucky Girl
Claire Hansen

OCCUPATION: Graphic Designer
LOCATION: Brooklyn, NY

It takes a woman with a distinct perspective on getting dressed to say that a pair of teal and hot pink floral silk-screened sandals goes with everything in her wardrobe. And Claire Hansen is the kind of person who can say it, mean it, and never look over-the-top when she does make those sandals go with everything. Hansen, a graphic designer, draws from a rich array of inspirations—old movies, Irene Dunne, bebop jazz—to create a look that is a unique blend of thrift-store chic, Old Hollywood glamour, and urban sleekness.

Her aesthetic emerged out of necessity. "I grew up in Virginia, in a Navy town, and didn't have access to designer clothing or mainstream stores, but there were amazing vintage boutiques," she says. "I'd show up to homeroom in Katharine Hepburn pants, pumps, and a fedora."

Hansen loves fitted '40s- and '50s-inspired pieces, unusual colors and patterns, and anything one of a kind. "I only have jewelry with stories attached, like a charm bracelet that I've been adding to since I was a child." And she still loves a good thrift-store find: "I never spend over $100 on anything."

Claire's Favorites

Stores: Tokio 7, Housing Works
Thrift Shops, D.L. Cerney
Online store: sundancecatalog.com
often has boots and shoes that I
very much want.
Movies that inspire my style:
Irene Dunne's sheer jacket in *The
Awful Truth*; Claudette Colbert's
suit in *It Happened One Night*;
Deborah Kerr's evening dress in
An Affair to Remember; and, of
course, Katharine Hepburn's
wardrobe in any number of roles.
**What I listen to while getting
ready for a night out:**
Jerry Lee Lewis, Gene Vincent,
Don Gibson, or Dolly Parton
Signature scents: Lily & Spice by
Penhaligon's is a wonderful one,
and Kiehl's musk oil is tried-
and-true.

From Claire's Closet

1.
Black-and-gold silk bustier top
I bought this at an Episcopalian thrift store. It looks really fantastic under sheer tops.

2.
Sheer ivory sleeveless dress with floral pattern
I bought this French hand-knotted linen lace dress from a vintage store in the East Village. This dress is very sentimental. I wore it to my dear friend Rebecca's wedding and gave the toast in it.

3.
Mustard polka-dot silk scarf
I found this scarf in a junk store in upstate New York when I was apple picking. I like to knot it around my neck. It's nice and thin, so it almost works like a tie or cravat and doesn't look bulky.

4.
Beige pleated polka-dot skirt
I think this skirt is so lovely—very *Roman Holiday*—with the wide waistband and the beautiful cream-and-brown palette. It makes me feel ultra-feminine and ballerina-like as I go about my city life.

5.
Vintage blue enamel butterfly earrings

This was the first purchase I made with the money I earned from my first job. I was 12 years old and worked as a page for the Virginia House of Delegates in Richmond. I spent three months living in a hotel. I found these inside a poky old junk store when I was exploring the city. I loved them then and I love them now.

6.
Cream silk top with black-and-red pattern

I wear this top once a week. It's my favorite piece of clothing. It has a Deborah Kerr–esque neckline, an interesting '40s print, and it's made of high-quality silk with covered buttons. I think it's timeless.

7.
Brown alligator-embossed leather skirt

This skirt is, oddly enough, seasonally adaptable. It looks great with tights, but it's still fairly cool to wear in warmer weather.

8.
Frye brown motorcycle boots

I like these with pants and short skirts. I got them for a third of their original price at the Sundance outlet in Salt Lake City, Utah. Love them!

"I'm more comfortable dressing down a bit for fancy events, and DRESSING UP FOR EVERY DAY. I like looking a bit different from the mood."

posh eclectic
putting it together

A hunting cape is super-elegant with flat-front pants and embellished flats.

Pair a vintagey polka-dot dress with dressy slingbacks for a slightly retro look.

In elegant black and white, a tiered lace camisole and sheer evening skirt are so, so pretty.

Don't be afraid to accent the deep neckline of a silk wrap dress with a rhinestone choker.

Cropped trousers are an interesting twist with a '20s-style blouse and heels.

A circle skirt, velvet jacket, and lace-up riding boots are ruggedly feminine.

**pink ruffled
skirt**

winter

Peeking out from under a houndstooth coat and over riding boots, the skirt is kicked-back glamorous and just as appropriate for city or country.

spring

Rich textures like lace, velvet, and metallic leather dress up the skirt without feeling fussy.

summer

For nighttime, echo the soft drape of the skirt with a delicate lace blouse and equally feminine accessories.

fall

Get a cozy, stylish weekend look by pairing the skirt with a Fair Isle sweater, black lace shirt, and vintage-style ankle boots.

Lucky Girl

Joan Wolkoff

OCCUPATION: Writer and Illustrator
LOCATION: Brooklyn, NY

"I like watching the way women evolve, especially between the ages of 16, when you start to buy things yourself, and your early 30s, when you've settled into a certain groove," says writer and illustrator Joan Wolkoff, whose own look has evolved from thrift-store-anything-goes into something that is at once both refined and eccentric.

These days she favors tweedy shades of gray, green, and brown and prizes a tailored fit above anything else. "I've learned the hard way that if it doesn't fit properly, even if you love it, you'll probably never wear it," she says. Focusing on the positive is a priority as well: "Even under casual conditions, I always like to accentuate both the narrower and broader points of my body, so when I want to look a little sexier, I'll wear something like a full skirt with a nipped waist and then a sweet, simple, flimsy blouse tucked in. But I'll never show a lot of skin."

At night, she says, she lets her wild side out: "If I'm feeling really outgoing, I'll wear jewelry improvised out of twine and found objects, lots of kohl around the eyes, and white canvas sneakers that I can dance in."

Joan's Favorites

Style era: Fashion in kitchen-sink dramas of the '60s
Style icons: Louise Brooks during her tantrum backstage in *Pandora's Box* or Pam Grier in *Sheba, Baby*
Movie that inspires my style: Terrence Malick's *Badlands*
What I listen to while getting ready for a night out: Paul Simon's *Graceland*
What's worth the investment: A well-made pair of shoes, quality bras, and having something tailored
Signature scent: Gris Clair by Serge Lutens
My number-one fashion rule: There's a time and a place for everything.

"I like **HERMÈS AND FERRAGAMO SILK SCARVES.** I'll spend hours searching through sidewalk sales and flea markets to find what I like."

From Joan's Closet

1.
Robert Normand white tank with snake-key print
Robert Normand's prints are always witty and mordant, and he works with wonderful silhouettes. He is my favorite French designer. His subversive spirit and eye for pattern make for some irresistible pieces!

2.
Brown leather sandals
These are sturdy and have a western-inspired, burnished look to them.

3.
Silk and velvet scarf with peony motif
The sensuality of silk and devore velvet is wonderful against the skin, and I like the idyllic, pastoral colors and lines of the motif.

4.
Purple paisley skirt
The print has been deconstructed like an impressionist painting. The nipped waist makes for an alluringly feminine silhouette.

5.
Art deco locket
I caught my breath when I found this perfectly weighted piece at a Parisian rummage sale. It has a faintly religious look and, mercifully, is not made of real ivory in spite of its old-fashioned finishing.

6.
Silk high-collared blouse in black-and-red print

The subtlety of this print and the color palette ensure a clean, demure look, and the tiny black lacquered buttons are a fanciful detail.

7.
Art deco pin

This is winningly linear and enameled in sultry hues of violet— a sleek embellishment to any minimalist ensemble.

8.
Gold poison ring with unicorn

This ring reminds me of a passage in *The Notebooks of Malte Laurids Brigge* by Rilke, about young women standing before a unicorn tapestry and contemplating adulthood. The caged unicorn is a romantic image in mythology, and it looks wistful in these kinds of jewelry pieces.

9.
Alligator handbag

My father, with his perfect under-standing of my sense of humor, gave me this stylish and slightly macabre purse. It is such a bold piece that I wouldn't dare wear it with anything other than a black linen suit.

posh eclectic
one piece, two ways

Job Interview
ruffle-front blouse + cropped trousers + bow-tie heels

Cocktail Party
ruffle-front blouse + lace skirt + red ankle-strap heels

posh eclectic
smart shopping

Take chances at the flea market

You need to have a Portobello-market mentality when shopping for the chic mishmash of Posh Eclectic. Train yourself to be good at scouring flea markets and looking at "funny" things differently. Something crazy—like an old, slightly run-down sequined top—would look amazing peeking out from under a cashmere cardigan or a tweed blazer. Be creative.

Search in fabric stores

If you can't afford a fur (or fake fur) collared coat, or you can't find one you love, fabric stores are great resources for understated, not-too-expensive strips of fur that you can add on to a coat you already have. Also, check out trim stores and websites for other extras like velvet ribbon, lace trim, and funky buttons for great additions to your outfits.

Buy vintage lace

New lace is often synthetic and cheap-looking. Look for lace labeled Bobbin, Chantilly, Needle, and, oddly enough, Machine Lace, which sounds very '80s prom dress, but has actually been around since the early 1800s.

Shop in simple outfits

This is a general rule of thumb that is especially important for flea market and vintage store shopping: Don't wear a complicated outfit. A giant coat, belted jeans, or lace-up shoes, for example, are a pain to yank on and off in small spaces or in front of people.

Pick comfortable Wellies

Wellies, believe it or not, are not always comfortable. Neoprene lining helps, but before you make your purchase, walk around in them a bit and make sure they don't rub your legs.

posh eclectic
store guide

Albertine: Situated in the parlor of a tree-shaded townhouse, Kyung Lee's shop has an old-fashioned aesthetic, from the teardrop chandeliers and delft-tile fireplace to the silky dresses and vintage fashion books. There's also an excellent collection of jewelry, which includes rose-cut diamond rings from estate sales, legitimately ancient intaglios that have been mounted into pendants, and reworked charm necklaces from up-and-coming designers. **New York, NY, 212-924-8515, albertine-nyc.com**

Barbour: A staple for the English hunting set (each of their waxed canvas Bedale jackets comes equipped with a back pocket for holding freshly shot fowl), Barbour has in recent years started cutting more figure-flattering shapes as well. **barbour.com for locations**

Cabbages & Roses: Lesser known—but for our money a bit fresher than fellow Brit textile designer Cath Kidston—interiors stylist Christina Strutt designs her feminine floral prints from a cottage in the Bath countryside and has them crafted into billowy tops and Peter Pan–collared dresses. **London, England, 442073527333, cabbagesandroses.com**

Doyle & Doyle: Specializing in estate and antique jewelry, this beautifully curated shop (with an equally enchanting e-commerce site) has uptown-quality pieces with a downtown sensibility: Look for everything from seed-pearl studded barrettes to art deco engagement rings. **New York, NY, 212-677-9991, tias.com/stores/doyledoyle/**

Equestriancollections.com:
Every few years or so, the runways are packed with some iteration of the riding jacket, and this is where we go for an affordable version. There's also a host of subtly elegant boots—and, if you dare—jodhpurs.

Madley: Raised in a Northern California log cabin and educated at famed London art school Central Saint Martins, Coryn Madley has an eclectic pedigree that is reflected in the fantastical magpie vibe that holds sway here: Sequined felt teardrops dangle from the ceiling, and a happy jumble of clothing graces the racks. **Venice, CA, 310-450-6029, madley.com**

Loopy Mango: This lofty spot has the lost-in-time quality of a grandmother's attic, packed with discoveries like silk-fringed velveteen lampshades, cobalt-glass perfume atomizers, duchesse satin blouses, and corseted wool dresses. **Brooklyn, NY, 718-858-5930, loopymango.com**

Mayle: Carefree, French-vintagey pieces are mainstays at Jane Mayle's only freestanding store—which is like a beautiful and well-traveled great-aunt's walk-in closet. High prices are justified by the gorgeous fabrics and careful tailoring, which lend pieces a handmade quality. **New York, NY, 212-625-0406, mayleonline.com**

Paris 1900: With arguably the largest selection of antique lace clothing in the country, this 30-year-old institution feels a bit like you've wandered into the middle of a wedding cake. But the pieces are stunning and unique: Intricately worked blouses, monogrammed shawls, and crocheted purses are all on offer. **Santa Monica, CA, 310-396-0405, paris1900.com**

Third Street Habit: Floral-fabric-draped dressing rooms, curlicue wrought-iron racks, and a velveteen love seat set an appropriately feminine mood at this much-praised boutique, favored for its forward-thinking assortment of clothing, which includes chiffon dresses from Swedish-based Dagmar and flatteringly loose, lightly patterned cardigans from Rodebjer. **Philadelphia, PA, 215-925-5455, thirdstreethabit.com**

Butik: A collaboration between old friends and fellow Danes, Helena Christensen—a former model (and Posh Eclectic poster girl)—and Leif Sigerson, this shop has the relaxed air of a rural cottage: Wispy lace Munthe plus Simonsen tunics and Faroe Islands–made crocheted camisoles hang on clothesline-like spans of rope. Everything has the feel of being one of a kind, because much of it is: You won't find these pieces anywhere else in the U.S. **New York, NY, 212-367-8014, butiknyc.com**

mod

When Mary Quant, the originator of Mod, began scribbling away in her sketchbook in the '50s, "there were these posters all over the subways with the slogan 'Brave New London,'" she once said. "And I used that as a directive for my designs." What she gave birth to was boldly black and white, zippered, geometric, and shiny—and went so far beyond new as to be positively futuristic. Consider Twiggy, who, in her stark black tights and white shifts, defined not just fashion but the cultural mood of an era. Mod still feels like the future—not the future as it happened but the era's happy, optimistic, and flirty version of it. Modern-day fans of the look, like Selma Blair, make a slightly less literal interpretation of it but couldn't be more appealing in their exaggeratedly tiny slice skirts and super-straight shifts. They look as sexy and stylish as possible, but this time around with a wink.

This page: Penelope Tree, 1964. Opposite page, clockwise from top left: George Harrison and Pattie Boyd, 1966; Zooey Deschanel, 2006; Twiggy, 1957; Cher, 1965; Yoko Ono, 1969; Selma Blair, 2007; Mary Quant, 1967.

essential pieces

black button-down shirt

cream silk blouse

boxy sweater

ankle-length
straight-leg jeans

gray schoolboy
trousers

sailor trousers

tie-neck
blouson sweater

pocketed smock
sweater

short-sleeved argyle
sweater

graphic cap-sleeved
blouse

embellished
evening top

three-quarter-sleeve
turtleneck

a-line skirt

brightly colored
miniskirt

knee-length
corduroy skirt

mod
essential pieces

patent leather
bomber jacket

collarless evening jacket

bright swing jacket

double-breasted coat
with fold-over collar

black-and-white
work dress

knit sweater dress

sheath dress with
big pockets

sequined minidress

trapeze dress

a-line minidress

white, black, and red
'20s-inspired dress

block-striped tank dress

mod
essential accessories

stack-heeled loafers

suede daytime
sandals

black-and-white
ballet flats

sleek flat black boots

vibrant yellow zipper
sandals

leather driving gloves

wide graphic belt

oversize
frame bag

patent leather
tote bag

white leather
handbag

envelope clutch

colorful enamel cuff

riding cap

oversize gemstone necklace

graphic earrings

metal disc
earrings

how to get the look

FIT AND STYLING:
The Perfect Boxy Jacket

This clean yet funky piece is a must-have for any Mod closet. Our favorites have funnel collars, slash pockets, and wide, slightly cropped sleeves. Look for the following details when searching for the right one:

- **Crisp tailoring. It should fit neatly at the** shoulder and hang straight down along your body in a clean, unbroken line to the hip. It should be very clean, almost utilitarian in feel. Because of its simplicity, it works for both day and night.

- **Smooth, uniform fabric such as linen,** gabardine, or silk; avoid anything that adds chunkiness, such as quilting.

Create Drama with Thick Stripes

Mod stripes are a different animal from nautical stripes: They're bolder, more graphic, and thick—between one and two inches—as well as evenly spaced, in rich, clean black and white. Loose-fitting, clean-lined dresses and tops make it easier for most people to pull off such a strong, high-contrast pattern.

How the Turtleneck Should Fit

You want this to have a little give—not so fitted that it shows your curves, but not so loose as to make you appear shapeless. And the neck itself should be wide: You should easily be able to fit one finger in each side. The fit on this piece is roomier all around, and the fabric shouldn't be ribbed—stick to a flat knit in cotton or wool.

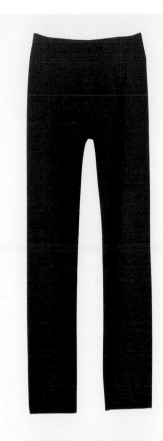

Pick the Right Shoes for Miniskirts

Super-minis should be *sold* with the right shoes. They're the essential balance and the reason why girls like Pattie Boyd and Twiggy looked so totally spot-on. Flat boots, high-heeled loafers, sensible, round-toe pumps with old-fashioned buckles and hardware—they're absolutely integral to wearing the super-mini.

The Best Cut for Ankle Pants

These should look like flat-front, schoolboy pants that are ultra-slim-fitting, but not tight or stretchy. The waistline should hit an inch above your hip bone, and the leg should be tapered and hit right at the ankle. Choose traditional and crisp-looking fabrics such as lightweight wool or gabardine, and in gray, black, pinstripes, or checks.

how to get the look

A Statement Coat Is Big, Bold, Mod Fun

Its shape should echo the clean lines of the A-line minidress (see next page). Black and white is wonderfully graphic, but a bright solid color is great for special occasions. Also look for cute details like oversize buttons or a tiny Peter Pan collar. The length should be just a bit longer than most of your skirts or dresses so that when you throw it on over a dress with some black tights and shoes, it looks like it could be a dress itself.

MUST-HAVE SHOE:
Flat Boots

These should look absolutely sleek and stovepipe-shaped, not too rugged or chunky, but not so fitted that you can see the outline of your calf. They shouldn't be completely flat-soled, but rather have a classic half-inch heel.

ICONIC ITEM:
The A-Line Minidress

What's so brilliant about this piece
is that it's flattering on almost everyone, it's truly easy to dress up
or down, and it layers well with tights and turtlenecks. It should be short,
with the hem hitting mid-thigh (though it works just as well anywhere above
the knee), and fitted at the shoulder and chest—it's not a tent dress. Other than that,
anything goes in terms of prints, colors, necklines, and sleeves. As long as
you've got the basic silhouette, you've got the look.

mod
Lucky Girl
Erika Forster

OCCUPATION: Singer/Keyboardist
LOCATION: Brooklyn, NY

"I love the look of the women in those Roger Moore–era James Bond films, when fashion wasn't taken so seriously and people could be more quirky—big hair, short, funny dresses with collars, and colorful tights," says Erika Forster, who is one-third of the Williamsburg, Brooklyn–based band Au Revoir Simone. "I like clothes that look like you could wear them to a party."

Offstage and on, she leans toward classic Mod silhouettes. She can frequently be found in short smock dresses with bright tights and low-heeled shoes—also quite Mod and, because she is almost six feet tall, practical. "I love old Hush Puppies," she says. "They're cute and comfortable and kind of go with everything."

Forster recently returned home after a year and a half of touring and found herself missing the fun of getting dressed up every night with her bandmates. "They're like my sisters," she says. "We'll all pile out of the van in some random town dressed up to the nines, and people will turn and look at us. I love that."

Erika's Favorites

Stores: Edith Machinist, Some Odd Rubies, A.P.C., Jumelle, Mayle, Shoe Market, H&M, American Apparel, Barneys New York

Online store: eBay

Style era: The '70s

What I listen to while getting ready for a night out: Lavender Diamond's *Imagine Our Love*

What's worth the investment: Boots, Wolford stockings, a great coat

I can't live without: A closet full of party dresses. And my vintage black leather jacket that I've had since I was 19

Signature scent: Pour Un Homme by Caron

From Erika's Closet

1.
Short-sleeved A-line silk dress

Navy is my favorite color to wear—it's so versatile. I bought this at Some Odd Rubies on the Lower East Side—it has all these gorgeous silk dresses by Miranda Bennett, which are great for travel because they pack up tiny.

2.
Cream leather ankle boots

I wear these onstage because I love the way the color really pops against bright tights.

3.
Black vinyl handbag

Kind of glossy and sleek and French.

4.
Susan Bijl peach-and-orange nylon tote

These bags were really popular in Japan, when we did our first tour there. I'm a big fan of fun, unusual color combinations—this looks like fruit or something.

5.
High-waisted wide-leg jeans with brass zippers

These are my favorite jeans—they're cut in this magical, flattering way. I like to tuck in bright T-shirts and tank tops to get an unusual silhouette.

6.
Elizabeth Yarborough
yarn-covered cuff bracelets
I knit and crochet, and I love these woolly bracelets. Even though they're funky, they're very clean and simple. I wear them when I get dressed up for night.

7.
Silver and braided
leather ring
I wear rings every day, and I like to collect all sorts of them from vintage shops and flea markets. This one has a lovely earthy feel but it's still super-graphic.

8.
Black leather
multistrap flats
These are comfortable, and I like that they have three straps as opposed to the typical single strap—it's a cool something extra.

"I love fabrics with **LOTS OF COLORS AND PATTERN,** a little Scandinavian-looking. They're very '60s."

putting it together

A simple sheath dress with flats and a frame bag says Mod without screaming it.

Offset an argyle sweater and a corduroy skirt with zippered, patent-leather sandals.

A trapeze dress looks pulled-together with matching heels and a smart white bag.

A navy blouson sweater and sailor trousers are perfectly punctuated by red flats.

The patent leather bomber jacket is an unexpected foil for an A-line skirt and flats.

Flat black boots toughen up a flirty tank dress.

black
stovepipe
pants

winter

Absolutely sexy—without being revealing—thanks to the right mix of a cropped fisherman's sweater, long coat, and tall boots.

spring

Stand out with a clean-lined shell, boxy jacket, and sandals all packed with unabashedly vibrant colors.

summer

Pants like these are the perfect way to keep a fun combination of a sequined tunic, silver sandals, and a graphic necklace from being too dressy or bare for a night out with friends.

fall

The timeless lines of a sailor blouse, double-breasted jacket, and big purse transform simple pants into an elegant, fresh cocktail party outfit.

mod
Lucky Girl
Annamarie Ho

OCCUPATION: Artist
LOCATION: New York, NY

Annamarie Ho is that enviable kind of woman who knows exactly what works for her. "I love wearing white in the winter because not many people wear it then," she says. "I have a big white coat that I like to throw on when the rest of my outfit is black." In fact, her whole closet is filled almost entirely with black, white, and navy— with a careful edit of graphic patterns and animal prints thrown into the mix for texture. Ho prefers vintage shoes, gold jewelry, and bags that have only gold hardware. "I like to dress clean," she says.

Ho's wardrobe consists of short skirts and dresses, very skinny or very wide-leg pants, and black tights. "For night especially, I love to have the focus be on black tights and a stunning pair of high-heeled black shoes. That's all you need to stand out."

All these precise, clean elements make for Ho's very glamorous, very current spin on Mod—lots of extremes combined beautifully with lots of minimalism. Her dream item of clothing, she says, is Catherine Deneuve's black patent leather trench coat from the movie *Belle de Jour*. "I've been fantasizing about it since the first time I saw the film when I was 14!"

Annamarie's Favorites

Stores: Balenciaga, Opening Ceremony, Project No. 8, H&M
Online store: eBay
Style era: The '60s
What I listen to while getting ready for a night out: My boyfriend, Dominique, produces music and DJs, so a mix by him usually does the trick. He's worked with bands like the Scissor Sisters, so it's usually some combination of dance and disco.
What I do to stand out at parties: I always make sure to wear only one exceptional piece and keep the rest simple.
What's worth the investment: A good haircut!
Signature scent: L'Eau d'Issey by Issey Miyake—I've been wearing it since I was 18.

From Annamarie's Closet

1.
Black-and-beige sleeveless knit dress

The back of this dress is spectacular: It has two twisted straps that crisscross and a cut that plunges quite low. I usually wear it with a thin belt to give it more of a defined waist.

2.
Gold basket-weave ring with red stone

This is vintage and comes with six interchangeable "stones," which are actually dome-shaped pieces of plastic. Each one is a different color—white, red, green, turquoise, navy blue, and amber—and I change them depending on the outfit I'm wearing. Sometimes I match the color to the outfit; sometimes I pick a color that stands out from a monochromatic outfit.

3.
Black suede knee-high boots

I've had these boots for several years now, and I continue to wear them winter to winter because they're so versatile. They can be worn three ways: over the knee, below the knee and folded, or slouched down.

4.
Black silk short-sleeved dress with ruffled hem

I adore this dress because it's so ladylike, with a high neck, a bow at the collar, and made of a beautiful silk. But the short, asymmetrical hemline keeps it modern.

5.
White carved ivory bangle and white beaded necklace

These two items are a set and are made of carved ivory. They were a present given to my mother on her 21st birthday, and she recently passed them on to me.

6.
Black leather miniskirt

I love the styling on this skirt—it's refined without being too tarty or '80s-looking. My favorite way to wear it is with a navy-and-gray-striped cashmere sweater, opaque black tights, and high-heeled black booties.

"I never wear more than ONE PIECE OF CLOTHING THAT IS TIGHT OR REVEALING, or else the whole outfit ends up looking trashy. If I wear fitted pants, then I make sure my shirt is not; if I wear a short skirt, then I wouldn't wear a low-cut blouse."

Outdoor Lunch
chiffon shell + **graphic black skirt** + mary janes

After-Work Drinks
striped sweater + **graphic black skirt** + heeled boots

smart shopping

Make sure it's matte

Completely black, matte opaque stockings are hard to find, but they're key to achieving the Mod look. Spanx makes great matte stockings that are reversible (black on one side; brown, blue, or gray on the other), which, for some reason, makes them that much more matte.

Secure your shoes

It's easy for feet to slip out of low-heeled shoes, especially when wearing tights. Get heel grippers for the backs of your shoes to help keep your feet in place.

Don't forget the lining

Cotton or twill dresses and skirts will cling to stockings, so look for ones that are lined or made of a smooth, mid-weight fabric that keeps its shape but doesn't bulk up.

Worth the investment

Mod is a look that's pretty constant and simple in feel—never too casual or too dressy—but a really great bag is the ideal way to step it up a bit. On our short list for expensive-but-worth-it is one in high-quality patent leather, a big-name designer style with oversize Mod hardware (Marc Jacobs, Chloé), or a fantastic straight-from-the-'60s vintage one like Roberta di Camarino or Courrèges.

Pick the perfect white

Walk into a paint store and you'll see that there's no such thing as straight-up white—there's ivory, snow, moonlight, you name it. Normally we wouldn't get specific about shades, but with Mod, the right super-bright white does make a difference. It's called "Optical white." Optical white should be whiter than white. It should *glow*.

mod
store guide

Kiitos Marimekko/ Marimekko: While at first glance these sister stores don't seem to have anything in common—one is an eensy boutique on the Upper East Side, the other is a large emporium in the South—they're both devoted to Finnish textile line Marimekko's greatest hits. Here, the famous oversize polka dots and boldly hued florals are available in dresses, Wellies, and smock tops. **New York, NY, 800-527-0624, kiitosmarimekko.com, and Oxford, MS, 800-926-2701, finndixie.com**

Frock: This basement-level vintage store has a certain insidery appeal, and it's easy to see why it's won so many loyalists: Here's where to go for spot-on pieces by mostly French designers like Courrèges and Pierre Cardin. **New York, NY, 212-594-5380, frocknyc.com**

Girls Love Shoes: Owned by two sisters, this vintage-footwear showroom (the duo has an archive of more than 3,000 pairs of shoes from the '30s to the '90s) stocks loads of Mod shapes from the '60s, like brilliant red flats from Salvatore Ferragamo and pilgrim-buckle-topped kitten heels by Maud Frizon. Their e-commerce site is especially compelling. **New York, NY, 917-250-3268, glsnewyork.com**

Penelope's: Cheeky vintage-classroom decor—checkerboard tile floors, antique school maps—lends a dose of nostalgia to this Wicker Park favorite. This is Mod reinvented for a generation of twentysomethings enchanted by all that is bright and cropped and sharp. Classic cuts, clean lines, and quality tailoring turn up in American Retro smocks, Dunderdon jackets, and Spring & Clifton crewneck sweaters. **Chicago, IL, 773-395-2351, penelopeschicago.blogspot.com**

Hus: Though Mod was a British invention, it's impossible not to see how greatly it was influenced by Scandinavian design—a point that is made particularly clear upon encountering this bright, spare space where everything on offer is either from Sweden, Finland, or Norway, including pop-y Tjallamalla dresses, Tretorn low-tops, and Filippa K blouses. For those looking to complete the lifestyle, there are housewares and men's and children's clothing on offer as well. **New York, NY, 212-620-5430, husliving.com**

Sigerson Morrison: Season after season, designers Miranda Morrison and Kari Sigerson serve up a satisfyingly broad range of patent leather flats in both neutrals and super-fun brights. (Check out their lower-priced sister store, Belle, for a slightly younger take.) They also offer the kind of knee-high, vintage-inspired flat boots that look like they could have walked off the set of *Quadrophenia*. **New York, NY, 212-219-3893, and Los Angeles, CA, 323-655-6133, sigersonmorrison.com**

Tibi: Marked by a tropical green, palm-frond-painted interior, this design house does A-line minidresses and skirts particularly well. The palette is also retro-inflected: One can usually count on an abundance of vibrant florals, geometric prints, and bold shots of color. **New York, NY, 212-226-5852, tibi.com**

Trina Turk: With a nod to '60s Palm Springs, Trina Turk reliably turns out impeccably cut minidresses and blouses, awash in deep oranges and pinks, lattice prints, and oversize florals. **New York, NY, 212-206-7383, and Los Angeles, CA, 323-651-1382, trinaturk.com**

Welovecolors.com: Tights are essential for any Mod outfit, and We Love Colors has hit the legwear trifecta: Its versions are absolutely opaque; are woven of matte, snag-free microfiber; and come in a spectrum of 45 hues. In addition to which they run just $12.50 per pair.

Built by Wendy: Indie designer Wendy Mullin churns out appealingly Mod-influenced designs, like mint green Peter Pan tops, window-pane-printed vests, and bell-shaped peacoats with oversize brass buttons. **builtbywendy.com for locations**

american
classic

The most timeless—and certainly most trendproof—of looks, American Classic is one that gets right at the heart of our collective fixation on the northeastern-elite lifestyle—a fascination that has held sway since we encountered Fitzgerald's Daisy Buchanan. Today that means something that's equal parts equestrian, Ivy League, and Jackie O–ladylike, but with a bit of urban knowingness thrown in as well. Think for a moment of Lauren Hutton in the early '70s: tawny, flawless, and ruthlessly sexy in a white blouse, navy blazer, and khakis. As Hutton so aptly illustrated, the look can be menswear-inspired without being unfeminine. (See also: Katharine Hepburn.) And—as coolly demonstrated by Lauren Bacall in her similarly clean-cut uniform—it can be elegantly spare. "I love understatement," Bacall once said. "I would go for a black suit any time. Put a ruffle on me and I'm done."

This page: Grace Kelly, 1956. Opposite page, clockwise from top left: Lauren Hutton, 1970; Jackie Onassis, 1970; Kelly Klein, 2004; Lauren Bacall, 1969; Mariel Hemingway, 1979; Carolyn Bessette-Kennedy, 1999; Katharine Hepburn, 1942.

american classic
essential pieces

classic denim
jacket

leather aviator
jacket

two-button
beige blazer

fine-ribbed
corduroys

dark-rinse
straight-leg jeans

cropped
white jeans

slim turtleneck
sweater

shawl-collar
cable-knit cardigan

summer party dress

bias-cut satin gown

simple black dress

embellished evening sheath

american classic
essential pieces

menswear coat

fur-collared parka

belted down vest

button-front
sweater top

collarless quilted jacket

double-breasted
weekend jacket

lightweight beige cardigan

v-neck sweater vest

oversize grandpa cardigan

boy's white t-shirt

fitted polo shirt

white button-down

narrow-fit
tweed skirt

a-line corduroy
skirt

high-waisted
pencil skirt

american classic
essential accessories

tassled high-heeled loafers

suede driving moccasins

sexy snakeskin heels

kitten-heel slingbacks

casual flat sandals

equestrian boots

crocodile day bag

overnight canvas bag

woven summer bag

strand of pearls

gold-link bracelet

round-face watch

diamond studs

pearl studs

silver and turquoise cuff

gold hoop earrings

gold knot ring

how to get the look

FIT AND STYLING:
The Perfect White Button-Down

If you own nothing else in this category, you must own a white button-down. Whether worn with jeans or a long taffeta skirt, it *is* American Classic. Here's what to look for:

- **A standard trim and hidden side seams**—avoid a version with seams darting down the front. Think prep-school uniform—plain and easy.

- **A beautiful quality fabric that's not too crisp**— a little softness keeps it sexy.

- **A pocket in the front is only for the office, while** no pocket can be worn for both work and play.

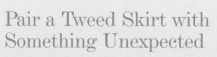

Pair a Tweed Skirt with Something Unexpected

When you want to look elegant, a tweed pencil skirt paired with a simple twin set always does the trick, but it works really well with a T-shirt, riding boots, and a jean jacket too, when you want something more relaxed. We like a tweed pencil skirt with a clean shape that falls at or just below the knee. Make sure there's little to no stretch in the material—the whole mood of a pencil skirt becomes more Bombshell when it's tight. Try offsetting the material with unexpected colors—it looks fantastic with lipstick red, for example.

American Classic Jeans

Think of Brooke Sheilds in the old Calvin Klein ads—these are trim and straight-leg with a rise that sits right above the hip bone. Choose a pair in a deep blue rinse and wear with a button-down shirt, sweater vest, and flats for a sophisticated weekend look.

The Right '40s-Style High-Waisted Trousers

They should have a swingy cuffed leg, belted waist, and a little crease down the front. For ultimate flattery, look for a mid- or lightweight wool that flows a little when you move and skims over the hip without looking bulky. The pleats should start below the hip. Offset the volume of the pants by wearing them with thin T-shirts, short-sleeved cardigans, or slinky tops.

A Great Balancing Piece

An oversize knit V-neck cardigan is perfect for throwing over any outfit that feels too sexy or too casual, like a bare-cut shift dress, say, or jeans and a T-shirt. Unbuttoned with the sleeves pushed up the elbow, the piece looks cute, not dowdy.

155

american classic
how to get the look

Knit Sweater Vests Are Preppy Cool

This is the ideal shortcut to a timeless collegiate *Love Story* freshness. Throw it on over a T-shirt and jeans, and you've got a just-pulled-together-enough Saturday outfit; wear it on its own with a short or mid-length fitted skirt and heels and it's sharp, and a tiny bit sexy. When choosing one, look for a true school-uniform fit, meaning loose enough to slide easily over button-down shirts, but not so loose as to be baggy.

THE ESSENTIAL:
Evening Shift

Spend money on a good shift dress: It will pay for itself in no time. You'll want one with a pared-down, fitted shape—not too tight, not too loose—and a skirt that narrows just a little at the knee. Look for simple necklines, tiny cap sleeves, or no sleeves at all, and just enough embellishment to give it some nighttime sparkle. Accessorize with only what's necessary—a clutch, heels, and gold hoops or diamond studs.

ICONIC ITEM:
The Blazer

American Classic is all about the blazer, the ultimate patrician piece
in corduroy or wool—or, for an American West, Ralph Lauren feel,
in leather or suede. It should fit perfectly at the shoulder, with
absolutely no pulling at the back. The hem should hit about
three or so inches past your hip, and the sleeves about two inches
past your wrist.

american classic
Lucky Girl
Alexa Levitt

OCCUPATION: NBC Human Resources Professional
LOCATION: New York, NY

When she first moved to New York from Washington, D.C., Alexa
Levitt admits, "I was very intimidated by how much style everyone
had. It was like everyone was *presenting* themselves. I basically
wore jeans and a sweater every day, but I finally said to myself, No
more cable-knit sweaters. No more baggy jeans."

Levitt then went about creating a look that she describes as
"much more sophisticated and feminine" than the one that preceded
it. "Now I do stuff like put a little '50s-inspired dress under a blazer
and wrap a big gold belt around the waist," she says. "I buy lots
of coats with voluminous collars—it's a simple detail that's so
chic. And peplum-shaped jackets, which are a nice combination of
tailored and girly."

Her job requires that she dress in a fairly corporate fashion,
but she tries to keep things interesting with pieces like a favorite
velvet blazer. And she's intent on never being viewed as a woman
who's trying to look like a "suit." "I never leave the house," she
says, "without my pink quartz and citrine rings—and of course
a fabulous bag."

Alexa's Favorites

Stores: Catherine Malandrino
and Saks Fifth Avenue
Style era: Now! I can finally
afford to buy amazing clothes,
and I am psyched that designers
are actually figuring out that
women need to look comfortable
and sexy.
Colors: Blues and greens, and the
NYC staple: black
Movie that inspires my style:
Kim Novak in *Vertigo*

From Alexa's Closet

1.
Nanette Lepore ivory
satin short-sleeved top
I like the elegance of ivory shades.

2.
Pomellato rose gold rings
with pink quartz and citrine
My parents gave me these
for my 30th birthday. I never, ever
take them off.

3.
Dolce & Gabbana
sunglasses
Big shades are so great when you
look a mess—they make everyone
look polished and glamorous.

4.
Prada oversize
black croc clutch
I never leave the house
without a big, understated
but rich-looking handbag.

5.
Seven for All Mankind
baggy jeans
My bumming-around-on-the-
weekend jeans. They are so,
so comfortable.

6.
Catherine Malandrino black strappy top
Crochet looks dressy and unusual in a low-key way.

7.
Alice + Olivia pants
I just love Alice + Olivia pants— they fit well and look sexy but still professional.

8.
Gold bracelet with lace snowflake charm
This is simple and pretty and a little nostalgic.

9.
Christian Louboutin pumps
I'd buy nothing but Louboutin high-heeled pumps if I could. They're the closest thing I've ever found to perfection.

10.
Magical Moon by Hanae Mori
This is my signature scent. It smells rich and exotic, but it's not overpowering. Plus, it lasts a long time.

"I love the versatility of button-downs— they're SUPER-ELEGANT, but they can also be unbuttoned and look really sexy for night."

putting it together

Pair a lightweight cardigan, pearls, and slingbacks with a structured, high-waisted pencil skirt.

Straight-leg jeans and a white button-down are sexy with strappy sandals.

For a retro-cute silhouette, wear a fitted polo T-shirt, an A-line skirt, and wedge sandals.

With corduroy pants and a
double-breasted jacket, try
menswear-detailed ballet flats.

Keep a little black dress
clean and simple with
elegant pumps.

An aviator jacket and riding
boots make an upscale tweed
skirt look sporty.

american classic
all year long

denim
jacket

winter

Worn under a camel coat and over a knit dress and knee-high boots, the jacket adds both an extra layer of warmth and a touch of ruggedness.

spring

With a refined polo, white jeans, and slingbacks, the denim jacket is just right for a laid-back night out.

summer

Make a feminine shirtdress and preppy canvas bag cool by adding the jacket and cinching the waist with an equestrian-style belt.

fall

Play up autumn's back-to-school mood and throw it on over a shrunken sweater with collegiate-classic trim trousers and a leather satchel.

american classic
Lucky Girl
Keisha Whitaker

OCCUPATION: Co-creator of makeup line Kissable Couture, Writer, TV Host

LOCATION: Los Angeles, CA

"I have 20 little black dresses," says Keisha Whitaker. But each one of them, she is quick to note, performs a very precise function in her wardrobe—as does everything else in there. "I work at my style," she says. "It's something I love and am constantly thinking about."

Whitaker's closet is full of the aforementioned dresses, perfectly tailored suits, and thin, stretchy T-shirts and tanks. She sticks to a mostly black, white, and cream color palette, with a little bit of wild thrown in—"I love red and animal prints," she says. "A little leopard-print heel peeking out under black Katharine Hepburn–style trousers makes such an impression."

For the red-carpet events she attends with her husband, actor Forest Whitaker, she stands out for her supremely elegant restraint. At a recent awards show, she wore a pale, fluttery gown, swept-back hair, and simple diamond studs. "I want to be wearing something that makes people look," she says, "but always makes sense."

Keisha's Favorites

Stores: Diane Merrick, Tracey Ross, Post 26, Marshalls, Target, Henri Bendel, Bergdorf Goodman, H&M, Scoop, Earnest Sewn
Online stores: net-a-porter.com
Style icons: Jackie O, Diahann Carroll, Dorothy Dandridge, Diana Ross, Audrey Hepburn
Colors: Cream, black, and white
Movies that inspire my style: *Mahogany*, *Breakfast at Tiffany's*, *Mommie Dearest*, and *Paris Blues*
Weekday uniform: Good jeans, a cashmere sweater, and hoop earrings

From Keisha's Closet

1.
Rosa Chá
black straw fedora
Rosa Chá makes this beautiful black straw fedora, with a little feather tucked in the band. I also love amazing wide-brimmed hats.

2.
Camel cashmere wrap
I'm addicted to cashmere—I love the way it feels. I put this on even when it's not cold out because the color is so beautiful. A cashmere wrap is the most versatile thing—it works as a blanket on the plane, an evening shawl when I'm somewhere warm, and bundled around my neck when it's freezing out.

3.
Chanel handbag
This is just exquisite—proper, dressy, and timeless.

4.
Brown knee-high boots
I can't live without a good boot. I like a high, '70s-style stacked heel, really fitted through the leg, and a bit distressed-looking.

"If you get a good pair of shoes and a great bag, you can wear JEANS AND A TEE every day, with nothing to prove."

5.
Black heels
I couldn't live without black pumps with very high heels. I never wear flats in the evening.

6.
Gucci suit
Tailoring is very important in a suit. There's nothing better than one that is cut and fit just for you. I wear my Gucci suit with a silky camisole or a great button-down shirt, but no belt, and some colorful patent leather heels for feminine balance.

7.
Paige Premium Denim skinny white jeans
I wear these every day. They're a narrow, slinky fit, and because they're white, it's easy to dress them up for night. They don't look like jeans. I'll add a white tank top, red patent leather heels, a great jacket, and I'm done.

Sunday Lunch
lightweight cardigan + wide-leg trousers + suede boots

Office Party
lightweight cardigan + full skirt + ankle-strap heels

smart shopping

Check fabric quality

To test the quality of a blazer, grab the wool on the back and hold for about 15 seconds—if you let go and it's still wrinkled, that means it won't bounce back from general wear and will be a mess at the end of the day. If the wool falls cleanly back into place, the blazer will look sharp when you wear it.

Pay attention to spacing

Carefully check the second button on a button-down blouse. Placement is key: A blouse can be frumpy and unflattering when it's buttoned, but it can also look inappropriate and revealing when it's open. In general, a button should hit mid-breastbone, and neither conceal nor reveal too much. Sit down in the dressing room when you try it on to make sure the front doesn't buckle and open up at the chest. If it does, wear a cami that's meant to show.

Stock up

If you find jeans you love, buy two pairs—one to wear with heels, and one to hem for flats.

Worth the investment

Only pure cashmere can be labeled 100 percent. Otherwise you might be getting a merino wool–cashmere blend, which isn't as soft or lush. That doesn't mean all blends are bad—we do like the thin, drapey look of silk-cashmere blends. A tightly woven knit is a good sign, but rub it a little with your hand to see if the fibers roll off. If they do, that usually means the piece will pill and fray easily.

american classic
Lucky Girl
Jillian McAlley

OCCUPATION: Photographer
LOCATION: New York, NY

"I'm very classic and minimalist, but I also want to be original with my style," says photographer Jillian McAlley, who manages to do just that by possessing a distinct fearlessness when it comes to matching the basics—skinny jeans, a cashmere sweater, Kate Spade rain boots—with an edgier piece like a studded, skull-buckle belt. And often, when McAlley wants to throw the mood of a straightforward look just a bit off-balance, she'll reach for a hat. "They're my signature," she says. "I feel like they're unusual enough to make anything I wear them with seem like an outfit." She rotates between Kangol caps, cashmere berets, and styles by Manhattan milliner Eugenia Kim.

As a freelancer, McAlley can wake up on any given day with—depending on the client—a new set of style demands. "What I think about when I get dressed is how the outfit will suit my day—especially when it comes to my shoes," she says. She rotates between Coach leather slip-ons, white canvas sneakers, and black Louboutin slingbacks. "Shoes are so important—they need to be comfortable, but they also need to be chic."

Jillian's Favorites

Stores: Annelore (for slacks, skirts, and jackets); Diane von Furstenberg (for dresses); Marc Jacobs (for shoes, bags, and accent pieces); Verve (for shoes); Theory (for essentials); Barneys Co-op (for fun finds)
Online store: bluefly.com
Movie that inspires my style: *Amélie*
What I listen to while getting ready for a night out: It depends on what kind of night out; it varies between Thievery Corporation, the Killers, and Pink.
What's worth the investment: Shoes, hats, and lingerie

From Jillian's Closet

1.
Diane von Furstenberg black-and-white patterned dress

When I saw this on the rack, I was immediately drawn to its classic design.

2.
Marc Jacobs brown leather bag

My husband surprised me with this bag after we had been dating for only a couple of months. It is just the right color and size.

3.
Christian Louboutin black heels

There are very few shoes that can make a woman feel sexier than 4¾" heels by Christian Louboutin.

"I've never felt more beautiful than on my wedding day, in a gown by Monique Lhuillier."

4.
Eugenia Kim brown hat

When I learned of Eugenia Kim's designs, I just *had* to own one. This is one of two of her pieces that I now have in my hat collection.

5.
Annelore long camel coat

I had the honor of shooting Juliana Cho's clothing line, Annelore, a few seasons ago. As a thank-you, she gave me this gorgeous tailored overcoat. It was a perfect fit!

6.
Diane von Furstenberg black dress

For a milestone birthday, I decided to invite my friends to dinner at [New York restaurant] Barbuto. A party dress was in order, so I treated myself to a sexy one by Diane von Furstenberg.

"When you buy **QUALITY TAILORED PIECES**—even if they're super-basic—they always look more elegant."

american classic
store guide

Looc: Authentic French sailor tees and Betta Carrano ballet flats are mainstays at this refined spot, which is co-owned by a veteran of Hermès and Ralph Lauren. The clothing palette is nearly neutral, and the white-walled space, accented with vintage luggage and croquet sets, is beautifully sparse. **Boston, MA, 617-357-5333, loocboutique.com**

Beanie + Cecil: With branches in Raleigh and Wilmington, North Carolina—appropriately centered at the nexus of southern university life—these popular boutiques specialize in bright and playful, just-fashiony-enough gin-and-tonics-oriented attire. There are dresses from Thread Social, eyelet blouses from Bell, and simple Loeffler Randall flats. **Raleigh, NC, 919-821-5455, and Wilmington, NC, 910-509-9197, beanieandcecil.com**

Brooks Brothers: Those looking to find a smart pants suit or perfect button-down shirt without spending a lot would do well to raid the boys' department here for what, on women, often turn out to be surprisingly great-looking pieces. **brooksbrothers.com for locations**

Filson: Established in Seattle in 1897 to outfit locals for the Klondike Gold Rush, Filson manufactured Mackinaw jackets, blankets, and moccasins. The company still churns out all manner of fishing and mountaineering gear, but what we love most is its excellent selection of muted green canvas luggage—everything from duffels with sturdy leather straps to simple totes. All the items are painstakingly well made and look far more expensive than they are. **Seattle, WA, 206-622-3147, and Denver, CO, 303-316-4406, filson.com**

J.Crew: Really, the bible of American Classic style. With reasonably accessible prices and an ever-more sophisticated—but still always approachable—aesthetic, it has also become the indisputable resource for certain items: We love the flat-front shorts, clean tanks, and impossibly thin, well-priced, summer-weight cashmere cardigans (which for our money are the best on the market). **jcrew.com for locations**

Holiday: Occupying a tiny space on Boston's quaint, boutique-lined Charles Street, this shop provides the unofficial uniform for a certain sector of the city's most pulled-together women. There are loads of tailored dresses in particular, from designers like Tory Burch, Lauren Moffatt, and Castle Starr. **Boston, MA, 617-973-9730, holidayboutique.net**

L.L. Bean: Long before the word "prep" became part of the fashion lexicon, this Maine-based institution was outfitting those who were actually battling the East Coast elements and participating in its sporting life. Now the catalog exists as a terrific resource for everyone looking to get the sporty look with all of the universal classics, from monogrammed canvas totes to boat shoes in kelly green and navy blue, and—for the truly hardcore—duck boots. **llbean.com for locations**

Lacoste: The alligator shirt has long been a staple of any preppy boy's or girl's closet, but this 75-year-old brand has in recent years taken an interest in attracting a more fashion-conscious customer in addition to its loyalists—while by no means abandoning its *sportif* roots. **lacoste.com for locations**

Ralph Lauren: Situated in the appropriately stately Upper East Side Rhinelander mansion and decorated with deep velvets and dark woods, the mothership for all things Ralph is arguably one of the most finely appointed stores in the country. (We're also quite smitten by Rugby, his young, irreverent clothing line that features cheeky spins on the classics, such as khakis embroidered with bitsy skulls.) **New York, NY, 212-434-8000, ralphlauren.com**

Gorsuch Limited: This is your resource for ski-town style with a Norwegian spin: classic Fair Isle sweaters and well-cut ski jackets are all on offer, as are some seriously Black Forest–meets-Aspen items for the home, including wall sconces mounted on antique snowshoes. The e-commerce site is excellent. **gorsuchltd.com for locations**

bombshell

"Sex appeal is 50 percent what you've got and 50 percent what they think you've got," said Sophia Loren. Bombshell just might be—depending on how far you choose to take it—the most labor-intensive look of all. These are women who work hard to get glamorous. They take care to slip on stockings so that the seam goes straight up the back; to cinch their waists way in; to wear coordinated lingerie sets, complicated corsets, and high heels—to the market. And isn't that refreshing? They take us out of time, away from trends and practicality; they exist as something luxurious and utterly feminine. Primarily '40s- and '50s-influenced—but not strictly vintage, as evidenced by Dita Von Teese's edgy allure—the core elements remain the same: It's about shape and it's about polish, with a dose of serious sparkle thrown into the mix.

This page: Sophia Loren, 1965. Opposite page, clockwise from top left: Marilyn Monroe, 1950; Dita Von Teese, 2005; Ann-Margret, circa 1960; Dorothy Dandridge, 1956; Scarlett Johansson, 2006; Kelly Osbourne, 2007.

structured halter top

lingerie-inspired camisole

corseted bustier

fitted capri pants

feminine high-waisted trousers

'40s-inspired pleated skirt

thin-knit
short-sleeved sweater

tie-neck chiffon blouse

fur-collared retro sweater

one-button
cardigan

velvet puff-sleeved
jacket

snug cropped
sweater

leopard-print pencil skirt

flared daytime skirt

ruched satin pencil skirt

bombshell
essential pieces

belted daytime jacket

evening swing coat

shawl-collar coat

retro-inspired
lingerie set

silk bra and tap pants

waist-cinching
corset top

satin evening coat

lace evening dress

sweetheart-neck
wrap dress

day-to-evening dress

fitted little black dress

polka-dot halter dress

bombshell
essential accessories

teardrop dangly earrings

sparkly deco brooch

delicate ladylike watch

big pavé studs

statement-making
cocktail ring

waist-cinching belt

houndstooth
day bag

structured
patent leather purse

silk-screened
frame clutch

patent leather
high-heeled mary janes

vintagey peep-toe heels

animal-print
d'orsay pumps

pastel slingbacks

satin platform mules

poufy party sandals

suede ankle boots

cloche felt hat

black leather opera gloves

bombshell
how to get the look

FIT AND STYLING:
The Perfect Hourglass Dress

This piece is essential to any Bombshell wardrobe. Look for these details:

- **A dark solid color and a** shape that's structured through the bust and nipped in at the waist.

- **A close fit through the hips** and a hemline that hits just at the knees or a few inches below.

- **An open, shapely neckline** (scoop, square, or sweetheart), rather than a high crewneck to keep the look sexy, not severe. Also, pass on any kind of fabric with shine to it. Study the knit a bit under the lights—this is when you'll really be able to detect it.

Making a Sheer Tie-Neck Blouse Work for You

Pairing this with anything high-waisted is a natural: Jeans, skirts, and trousers all look fantastic with a little blouse like this. Keep the fit quite narrow along the torso so that it tucks in smoothly and doesn't blouse out too much.

Bombshell Jeans

These are so '50s screen-goddess—think of Elizabeth Taylor in *Giant*. A capri-style cut like this should be tight but not uncomfortably so, with a flat front and a hem that hits just above the ankle and looks good with both flats and pumps. A mid-rise or high waist is best. Pick thin denim with a little stretch to it in a deep indigo rinse.

Add Drama with Opera Gloves

Stunning with short-sleeved coats and evening dresses, these elbow-length, thin, unlined black leather gloves add instant drama. They should be fitted enough so they cling to your arms and aren't baggy.

The Right Corset Top

It shouldn't look like actual lingerie (that's more early Madonna), so skip anything too silky or lacy. Ones that lace up the back send a different message—more Sexpot than Bombshell. A simple hook-and-eye closure up the front is cleaner and dressier.

bombshell
how to get the look

The Timeless Evening Jacket

An ultimate evening jacket should have classic glamour lines: a swingy, slightly trapeze shape that hits just above the hips; elbow- or three-quarter-length sleeves (to show off those long gloves); and an overall clean line. We love the delicacy of a single-button closure and rich, textured fabric. It's so stunning when you wear this during the day with cropped jeans—or at night with a full-length gown.

KEY ACCESSORY:
Vintage-Style Lingerie

Totally old-school and elegant in feel, pretty bras (with matching tap pants or bikini bottoms) are the beating heart of this whole look, whether or not anyone besides you sees them. You can't walk the walk without really fantastic lingerie on.

ICONIC ITEM:
The Pencil Skirt

High-waisted pencil skirts are ideal
for tucking tops into, which creates
the waist-accentuated style that
is essential to this look. Low-
and mid-waisted ones are trickier,
because having a shirt blouse
out at the hip looks a little off.
Also try wearing it with a cropped
sweater or a fitted jacket, or even
a cool T-shirt if you want to look a
bit edgier.

bombshell
Lucky Girl
Cori Bardo

OCCUPATION: Hairstylist
LOCATION: Los Angeles, CA

"I love that curvy sexy-secretary look," Cori Bardo says. "But at the same time, I was totally a punk rocker when I was a teenager, and even though I don't dress like that now, I still like to include an element of it in the way I dress. My style is like a battle between two worlds."

For the Los Angeles–based hairstylist, that manifests itself in a surprisingly smooth way: She keeps her look bombshell-bright and hourglass-curvy with a standard uniform of a high-waisted black pencil skirt or retro jeans, a vintage blouse, and a black leather bondage-style belt.

A big part of Bardo's look comes from her love of vibrant colors: "I like how dramatic they look on me because I'm so pale," she says. Her closet's full of dark purple, pale pink, and teal that she likes to mix with darker accent shades to keep things a little more modern. "I love wearing lipstick red with dark brown, fuchsia with navy, and pale pink with charcoal gray," she says. "It looks beautiful."

Cori's Favorites

Stores: H&M, Opening Ceremony, Curve, Presse
Online store: revolveclothing.com
Style icons: Bianca Jagger and Brigitte Bardot
Movie that inspires my style: *Atonement*
What I listen to while getting ready for a night out: Prince usually puts me in a good mood.
What's worth the investment: Boots and purses. Pants if they fit perfectly
I can't live without: Anything by my sister's line, Rose
Signature scents: I like to switch between Angel by Thierry Mugler, Miss Dior Chérie by Dior, and Bulgari Pour Femme.

From Cori's Closet

1.
Nanette Lepore chiffon top
The cut and peachy color of this top is very feminine, but the red beading adds a bit of cool, interesting texture. It's pretty long, so with wide-leg jeans and heels it makes a flattering, almost tunic-like silhouette.

2.
Gold cuff with pyramid spikes and chunky black cuff with gold spikes
These look good with casual or dressy outfits. I wear them with pretty much anything—even jeans and a T-shirt. They can truly make a plain outfit look stylish.

3.
Vintage lavender dress
It's unusual to find this color nowadays. It's a retro shade, and it fits me in the most amazing way.

"I love this purple Pinko jacket. I wore it to Fashion Week in New York."

4.
Black patent and metallic gold stiletto booties

I always wear heels—these are in between being really tough and really Bombshell and look just as good with a pretty dress as they do with jeans.

5.
18th Amendment high-waisted, wide-leg denim jeans

Hands down my favorite jeans— I have several pairs.

6.
Blumarine leopard-print chiffon tunic

I've always loved animal prints, but I can only do *one* leopard thing at a time. This looks great with a gray pencil skirt.

7.
Jimmy Choo handbag

I'm definitely a bag girl—I always buy a new bag when I should get a pair of shoes. My everyday purses are huge, practically duffel bags, but at night I like them small and glamorous. This deep blue evening bag doubles as a clutch if I tuck in the strap.

8.
Wide black braided-leather belt

I usually wear this very high on my waist over a vintage blouse, paired with either a skirt or tight jeans.

"I would love to **LIVE IN GOWNS** for the rest of my life. I love those romantic flowing ones that Keira Knightley wore in ATONEMENT."

putting it together

A sexy halter dress goes from poolside to evening with white wedges.

Simple capri pants balance out a structured top and leopard-print shoes.

A skinny pencil skirt is work-appropriate when paired with a belted jacket and peep-toe heels.

Add '40s-style sandals to a sweetheart-neck wrap dress for casual glamour.

Pair a corseted bustier with refined high-waisted trousers and chunky platform heels.

A leopard-print pencil skirt looks cool with a colorful, short-sleeved sweater and a clutch.

clean-lined corset

winter

Peeking out under a slinky blouse and paired with wide-leg trousers, the corset adds just enough sultriness for night.

spring

Worn under a nipped-in blouse, dressy jeans, and d'Orsay pumps, a corset provides that extra bit of sophistication that takes the look from day to night.

summer

Bare yet structured, it's the perfect party-time centerpiece—simply add a soft pencil skirt, strappy heels, and a sexy clutch.

fall

Go for old-school seductress with Bombshell basics—a leopard-print jacket, a pencil skirt, and platforms—that look modern, not vintage.

bombshell
Lucky Girl
Nissa Botthoff

OCCUPATION: Set Decorator/Prop Stylist
LOCATION: New York, NY

Nissa Botthoff's unabashed love of dressing up began with childhood visits to her grandmother's house. "My grandma was fabulous. She had perfect red nails and wore great jewelry every day of her life. I could have happily spent the rest of my life just standing in her closet, staring at her clothes."

Botthoff's look is composed primarily of fitted dresses, high heels, cinched waistlines, and classic colors. But what really makes her style so distinctive is her well-edited array of accessories. "I like little kerchiefs for the hair, with hoop earrings. Berets always look cute with a simple outfit—very Faye Dunaway in *Bonnie and Clyde*. I went through a phase of wearing only green high-heeled pumps."

She once found herself obsessed with finding a pair of gray suede high-heeled oxfords. "I had just come back from Paris, where all these chic girls had them. I was dying to wear them with a little bubble skirt and gray tights. So *Belle de Jour*."

Overall, she is not afraid to make a statement: "At night when most people are in black, I like to wear dreamy colors like blush and cream. Even if it's just a simple dress, it always stands out from the crowd."

Nissa's Favorites

Stores: H&M and Zara; Bloomingdale's and Anthropologie (for shoes); Saks Fifth Avenue (for eveningwear and the cashmere collection); sidewalk street vendors (for inexpensive, trendy jewelry)

Movies that inspire my style: There are so many: *Belle de Jour, 8½, Some Like It Hot, 2046, Twin Peaks, The Thin Man, The Umbrellas of Cherbourg, To Catch a Thief, Saturday Night and Sunday Morning, Roman Holiday, And God Created Woman, The Royal Tenenbaums, High Society, Blade Runner, Breakfast on Pluto, La Dolce Vita.*

What's worth the investment: A beautiful (and warm) coat

I can't live without: My grandma's knee-length cashmere wrap coat in pale oyster

Signature scent: Chanel No.5

From Nissa's Closet

1.
Valentino chiffon gown
Valentino is my favorite designer for all-out, old-school glamour. This dress reminds me of the gowns in Helmut Newton's photographs for French *Vogue* in the late '70s.

2.
Vintage floral-print dress
I'm very picky about the fit of my dresses—I have to have a fitted waist and shoulders, an open neckline, and a skirt that ends just above or below my knee. I usually only find the ones I really like in vintage stores.

3.
Rhinestone and jade brooch
I just adore jade and anything green.

4.
Rhinestone monkey brooch
I love animal jewelry. This piece is so Kenneth Jay Lane or Cartier (and *très* retro). The monkey is kind of exotic, but I also think it's funny to wear a monkey—in a fabulous, eccentric, old-lady kind of way.

5.
Chunky green bracelet
This is what a '50s starlet would bring back from her retreat in Acapulco.

"I have a kind of **OLD-FASHIONED NEED TO BE FINISHED.** My grandmother always told me that if you're outside after dark, your shoulders should be covered."

6.
Tevrow + Chase
fitted three-button blazer
The fit and tailoring on this jacket are impeccable and feminine.

7.
Wide brown belt
Adding this belt is the quickest and easiest thing I do to make an outfit unique. I cinch it over a fitted dress (it looks fabulous over prints) or pair it with a high-waisted pencil skirt. It's also a great way to perfect a dress that doesn't fit quite right.

8.
Black canvas tote with
white piping
Contrast piping on anything is poppy and graphic, yet elegant. Very nautically inspired.

9.
Navy patent
open-toe pumps
I think this is such a curvy, sexy shoe. I love navy. I don't own any black shoes or handbags. Shoes are not an afterthought for me. I want to showcase them when I'm dressed up, not just wear a pair that is safe and matches.

bombshell
one piece, two ways

Birthday Party
leopard-print blouse + purple skirt + pointy-toe pumps

Work Dinner
leopard-print blouse + black pants + ankle boots

bombshell
smart shopping

Buy in advance

Don't buy a glamorous dress the day you plan to wear it—that's the one day you're guaranteed not to find one. Alternately, if you come across a dress that suits you, buy it on the spot. Even if you don't have an event that night, the next I-don't-have-anything-to-wear occasion is always right around the corner.

Take advantage of department-store tailors

The Bombshell look is all about the perfect fit. Ideally you'd have everything altered just a bit, but that can be both expensive and time-consuming, so don't forget that many department stores have in-house tailors who will hem or nip for free, or at least for a very small fee. (But remember, once something's been tailored, you can't return it.)

Add vintage touches

An old flea market brooch or a pair of shoe clips can change plain black pumps into super-glam scene stealers. But before you buy, examine the backs of vintage jewelry for glue, chips, or anything that would suggest it's been "fixed."

Look at all angles

This is a very body-conscious look, and you've got to be totally honest with yourself when buying a super-snug piece of any kind. Check yourself out in a full-length mirror; if there is a three-way mirror, all the better. Step back as far as you can, and study yourself. It's amazing how different an outfit can look in a head-to-toe mirror versus a typical, compact, cut-off-at-the-knees style. Also, beware the sneaky slimming mirrors—a lot of stores have them.

bombshell
Lucky Girl
Mary Ta

OCCUPATION: Showroom Owner/Design Entrepreneur
LOCATION: Los Angeles, CA

"I'm a total extremist," Mary Ta says. "I just love visuals." Ta runs
two showrooms in L.A. for the posh Italian furniture company
Minotti, and her wardrobe is equally stunning—a beautiful combination of retro Paris glamour and satiny starlet luxury. "There's a
definite fantasy element to how I dress," she says. "I always throw
in something like a fur stole, a little cocktail hat with feathers and
a veil, or an Asian hair ornament."

What keeps her look modern is how she fuses those retro
influences with a design-heavy, innovative edge: a sharply ladylike ruffled black jacket made of thin leather; a wide waist-cincher
covered with intricate laser-cut details. "I love the way Sean Young
dressed in *Blade Runner*, especially her suits. They were so '40s-
inspired yet futuristic."

Ta is vigilant about the quality and cut of what she buys.
"I never shop for clothes online—I really need to handpick what
I buy. Overall, everything I wear is pretty exotic and rich. I always
look like I'm kind of dressed up for a party, even if I'm just
running errands."

Mary's Favorites

Stores: Kiki de Montparnasse
(for their beautiful lingerie);
L'Eclaireur; Pucci; Etro; Neiman
Marcus (for shoes); Curve in L.A.
(for young designers); Decades
(for vintage); J.Crew (for classics)
Movies that inspire my style:
Henry & June, *Dracula* with
Gary Oldman, *Blade Runner*,
The English Patient
**What I listen to while getting
ready for a night out:**
If I'm going to a party, then Scissor
Sisters' "I Don't Feel Like Dancin'"
or Trentemøller's "Moan." If I'm
going to dinner, I like Fairuz or
Maria Callas.
What's worth the investment:
Shoes—they define an outfit and
carry you all day.
Signature scent: Mughetto by
Santa Maria Novella

From Mary's Closet

1.
Dries Van Noten top
This is so unique, and the material is amazing—it's almost like a sculpture. I like to wear it with my slim black Gucci pants and my black diamond David Yurman ring. You don't need to accessorize much with great pieces like this.

2.
Pheasant headpiece
This is from Lords in West Hollywood, which is run by my ex-husband. They have one-of-a-kind headpieces and beautiful hand-tailored leather clothes made to order. I wear this when my hair is in a ponytail with bangs.

3.
Black leather opera gloves
I am an emotional dresser, so my moods inspire what I wear. When I am in a dramatic mood, I wear these gloves to spice up a simple cocktail dress. I also wear them with short-sleeved coats, like my white cashmere Marc Jacobs coat, which is '40s-inspired.

4.
Sergio Rossi natural leather boots
These are very soft and comfortable. I wear them with white riding pants and a navy satin blouse with ruffles. It's like an updated riding outfit with a modern-luxury feeling.

"On the way to Gregory Colbert's show ASHES AND SNOW wearing a custom-made silk chiffon dress by Valerj Pobega."

5.
David Yurman
black diamond ring

I wear this all the time. It's such a striking ring, but still subtle, elegant, and sexy.

6.
Gucci black dress

This dress is so versatile. I can wear it in the daytime with a nice light jacket, or I can make it sexy with black leather gloves. It's so figure-flattering and well-tailored.

7.
Purple lace leather cincher

I bought this in Milan two years ago at Gio Moretti, which carries a handpicked selection of great European designers that you may not find in the States. I adore this corset because it is sexy but sophisticated, and I can wear it day or night.

8.
Pierre Hardy
evening shoes

These have an alluring, elegant feel. I wear them with these stunning nude stockings with black seams on the back from Trashy Lingerie in L.A. and a short Burberry dress.

"The first thing I put on when getting dressed is shoes—USUALLY HEELS—because I think they define what the rest of the look should be."

bombshell
store guide

Meilleur Joaillerie: At this insanely boudoir-esque costume jewelry store—every wall is covered in toile, and chandeliers dangle from the ceilings—the cases are packed with surprisingly reasonably priced pieces, some of which come from area estates. There are drop earrings inset with turquoise, oversize cocktail rings, and pins covered in precious stones.
New Orleans, LA, 504-525-9815

Agent Provocateur: Ribbon bedecked knickers, lace corsets, and cherry-patterned bras are all mainstays at this British lingerie emporium, where hyper-sexy silhouettes are treated in a retroish and often arch—but still super-hot—fashion. Though there are outposts all over the world (including Heathrow Airport), the easy-to-shop website stocks it all. **agentprovocateur.com for locations**

Betsey Johnson: The reigning queen of punky/girly party clothes, Johnson is a fashion-for-the-people iconoclast who traffics primarily in dresses—from strapless polka-dot bubble numbers to floral cap-sleeved gowns. Her shops, with their hot-pink walls and leopard-print floors, reflect the designer's exuberance for pattern and color. **betseyjohnson.com for locations**

Electric Couture: In 2007, Phoenix-area stalwart Electric Ladyland became Electric Couture, an opulent venture that's awash with gold chandeliers and boudoir furniture. There's nary a piece of clothing that's embellishment free, from beaded blouses to rhinestone-adorned skirts, and the focus is on evening-centric lines like McQ–Alexander McQueen and Tom Binns Couture. **Phoenix, AZ, 866-948-9341, electriccouture.com**

Fille de Joie: Neon pink graffiti-style murals mix with rococo antiques at CC McGurr's Williamsburg, Brooklyn, vintage emporium, which is the go-to spot for Bombshell style with a downtown twist. Vintage picks from big names like Christian Lacroix, Chanel, and YSL share the racks with more obscure labels. **Brooklyn, NY, 718-599-3525, filledejoienyc.com**

Rhinestone Rosie: Proprietress Rosie Bryzelak Sayyah is one of the country's foremost experts on rhinestone jewelry—she's been collecting for 24 years and is an appraiser on *Antiques Roadshow*. Her chaotic shop drips with sparkly necklaces that start at just $25—arguably the best place in the country to get the most glitter for your dollar. **Seattle, WA, 206-283-4605, rhinestonerosie.com**

Trashy Diva: Trashy Diva specializes in '40s- and '50s-style waist-enhancing dresses by designer-proprietress Candice Gwinn that have earned a following for their ability to render just about any body curvy in all the right places. Its offshoot offers a carefully selected range of retro-styled underpinnings, including gracefully sweeping satin robes, Chantilly lace camisoles, and bias-cut pinup-girl slips. The old-school feel of both shops is reinforced by the vampy-glam furnishings, like enormous gilded mirrors and plush sheepskin rugs. **New Orleans, LA, 504-299-8777, trashydiva.com**

The Way We Wore: Legendary vintage dealer Doris Raymond—who outfits loads of starlets for big events like the Oscars—puts only the most trend-focused items on her sales floor, taking care to stock gowns that look glamorous and sexy, rather than like they stepped right off the set of a period piece. **Los Angeles, CA, 323-937-0878, thewaywewore.com**

Christian Louboutin: Even though every Christian Louboutin shoe comes with an impossible-to-miss signature red-bottomed sole, his teeteringly high stilettos—cut to make every foot look prettier than it's ever looked before—are unmistakably recognizable from the front too. **New York, NY, 212-396-1884, christianlouboutin.fr**

arty slick

"I look at clothes as if they are pieces in the Guggenheim," says actress Isabella Rossellini, and in its purest form, this fearlessly stylish look will forever be ahead of its time. Full of structured, asymmetrical jackets and dresses, layered tops with uneven hems, and boldly sculptural jewelry, this is about both avant-garde flair and minimalist cool. Almost everything is black, save the jewelry, and has some (very carefully chosen) twist to it: swingy draping; a collar with shape or volume; a V-neck that doesn't quite V. Still, for all its drama, Arty Slick isn't all or nothing; you can prove your point with slouchy trousers, a skinny tank, and a bright Maori-collar necklace. Either way, the key to making it work is to let go of any desire to blend in with the pack—like jewelry designer Tina Chow did when she wore frantically ruffled jackets and boys' T-shirts to Studio 54 while everyone else had on lamé hot pants.

This page: Isabella Rossellini, 1992. Opposite page, clockwise from top left: Anne Parillaud, 2003; Sadie Frost, 2003; Tilda Swinton, 2007; Björk, 1999; Donna Karan, 2008; Cecily Brown, 2005.

essential pieces

sweatshirt vest

faux-layered t-shirt

ragged-hem chiffon tank

drapey two-tone shift

deconstructed evening
dress

deep v-neck grecian dress

exaggerated
funnel-neck shift

sheer paneled
minidress

fluttery
asymmetrical tank

textured black tank dress

low-rise wide-leg trousers

black skinny pants

essential pieces

oversize distressed parka

funky layered coat

long double-zippered
cardigan

slouchy jacket

dramatically ruched
jersey top

structured
tuxedo jacket

off-center zippered hoodie

button-neck weekend sweater

tailored cardigan

bright batwing blouse

black-and-white
printed blouse

short-sleeved leotard

uneven pleated skirt

box-pleat skirt

cropped genie pants

metallic hobo bag

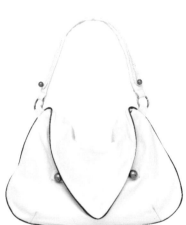

graphic white purse

slouchy patent leather bag

cutout-detail
ankle boots

leather and suede
pumps

ankle-band
sandals

knot-detailed necklace

industrial-style
metal choker

chunky mixed-material
necklace

utilitarian
lace-up boots

sculptural
silver earrings

cutout
black belt

oversize abstract
plastic ring

bright resin
cocktail ring

arty slick
how to get the look

ICONIC ITEM:
The Asymmetrical Top

You've got the look down with this easy, ideal
layering piece—even if you do nothing but wear
it under a sweater with an unexpected bit peeking
out of the bottom. The thinner and more fluttery
the material, the fancier the overall look. Since the
hem is not meant to be perfect, you might want to
customize an old T-shirt dress for yourself. Cut it
as long or short as you want.

KEY ACCESSORY:
Sculptural Jewelry

Statement-making pieces are what give this
look its interesting, creative edge. Look for pieces
that appear hand-wrought out of silver or bronze in
geometric shapes (cubes, discs, bars). An oxidized
finish is an extra unique touch, too.

The Right Side-Button Sweater

This gives an instant '80s street-urchin punkiness to any outfit. The collar buttons up like a turtleneck, but wear it open with the under-layers peeking out, like an art student.

Try an Off-Kilter Kilt

Be on the lookout for these: Designers make them suprisingly frequently. Keep the fit grown-up and fluid and always wear it sitting at the hip.

Fail-Safe Trousers

We love the look of soft menswear-style trousers that are exaggeratedly slouchy— they're arty and strong-looking, but not really that out there (after all, they're essentially just black pants). Think of these as a go-to basic—they go from day to night and work with every-thing else in your closet, from a white T-shirt to the fasci-nating blouse of your choice. Avoid skinnny high heels, which can easily get caught in the long, wide pant leg. Stick with flats, or if you want extra height, platforms.

Choose a Statement-Making Day Dress

This piece should be simple and loose, but with some unabashedly daring feature— a sculptural neckline, dramatic puff sleeves, oversize pockets. Take a less-is-more approach to choosing accessories—the dress itself is the statement. A minimal yet unusual sheath for day really anchors and transmits to the world what your style is without screaming it.

arty slick
Lucky Girl
Wayne Lee

OCCUPATION: Fashion Designer
LOCATION: Brooklyn, NY

"I always think too little is better than too much," says Brooklyn-based, Vietnam-born fashion designer Wayne Lee. "I wear the same thing almost every day."

Lee's taste for subtlety is what led her to a career in fashion design. While working as a buyer at Barneys New York, she frequently received compliments from customers and staff on the simple, yet eye-catching outfits that she wore to work. "I would design things I wanted to wear, and my aunt would sew them for me," she says. "People liked them and would ask me where I got them."

Lee favors basic pieces like jeans, T-shirts, shift dresses, and jackets with a touch of the unusual—origami pleats, zippered details, double collars, liquid fabrics like thin parachute silk, and a color scheme of white, red, and black. Fabric and texture are also very important. "I love how texture can make something casual look a little dressier, or a dressy thing look more casual. My favorite outfit to wear at night is a really sheer white T-shirt with tight, faded jeans, and black patent leather pumps. It's nothing fancy, and yet because the contrasting textures are artistic, it somehow becomes dressy."

Wayne's Favorites

Stores: Comme des Garçons, American Apparel, the flea market on West 25th Street in Manhattan, Two Jakes, and Ugly Luggage
Online store: zappos.com
Style era: The '40s
Style icon: Maggie Cheung in *Irma Vep*
Movies that inspire my style: *Blade Runner, Masculin Féminin, 8½, Stranger Than Paradise*
What I listen to while getting ready for a night out: Pixies' *Surfer Rosa*
Signature scent: Guerilla by Comme des Garçons
My number-one fashion rule: Never overdo it.

From Wayne's Closet

1.
Gold sequined dress
This is a fun dress to wear with a brown leather belt cinched high on the waist. I can dress it up with a pair of black pumps or down with white Keds. It reminds me of the sequined dresses my mom used to wear.

2.
White chiffon tank
I particularly adore this top. It's a wonderful layering piece. I like to wear it with a white cotton tank underneath with a pair of black men's slacks, jeans, or jean shorts.

3.
Chunky boyfriend cardigan
This is a staple of my wardrobe during the fall. It's great to layer with a coat or wear casually with an oversize white V-neck tee and loose black trousers rolled up.

4.
Black leather bag
The embossed leather of this bag is amazing. It's light and casual, and it's perfect with faded old jean shorts and an oversize T-shirt in the summer.

5.
Gold ring
My friend Peter made this, and it's one of a kind. I think the rawness and the gold are just beautiful.

6.
Silver lion ring
I love the silver lion head, which reminds me that I need to be courageous.

7.
Black leather jacket
The sleeves and body on this jacket are slim, and it fits me like a glove. I wear this with faded jeans and a sheer, oversize T-shirt or just a simple silk slipdress.

8.
Lanvin flats
These are super-comfortable and casual, and the nude color works with practically any outfit.

9.
White shorts
I am crazy about shorts! Maybe it's partly a result of growing up in Florida. These are silk, and they are great to wear with something casual, like a cotton tank, or to dress up with an oversize blazer.

"I wear my white leather Converse sneakers every day. THEY'RE PERFECT—comfortable, a little unusual, and they match almost all my outfits."

putting it together

The mixed-up moods of a sporty sweatshirt vest and a dressy kilt work seamlessly together.

In deep industrial shades, a drapey shift and strappy heels have just enough grittiness.

Pair a structured tuxedo jacket with a box-pleated skirt for an unexpected silhouette.

Offset skinny pants with a ruched jersey top, graphic heels, and a chunky necklace.

Make a metal choker the centerpiece with a black tank dress and muted slingbacks.

The chiffon tank and pointy heels are dressy—but cropped genie pants add a little edge.

**brown
jersey dress**

winter

Pair the dress with an equally drapey cardigan, structured coat, and ankle boots for a stylish and cozy weekend option.

spring

A bright printed coat, extra-funky heels, and a sleek handbag create the ideal mix of versatility and slink for a night out.

summer

Accessories that are a little bit special—touches of gold, graphic cutouts—transform the dress into a sexy-easy urban-goddess outfit.

fall

Add straightforward workaday pieces with an extra bit of shape to them to play up the simple-with-a-twist feel while still being office-appropriate.

arty slick
Lucky Girl
Gaelle Drevet

OCCUPATION: Co-owner, Pixie Market
LOCATION: New York, NY

"I went to a house party when I was about 18, and we had to take our shoes off at the entrance. I remember seeing my bright yellow shoes in a sea of black ones," says the Paris-born Drevet. "I thought, Hmm, I dress differently from other people." That love of the unusual led Drevet to leave her job as a television producer and, along with a friend, to open the Lower East Side clothing boutique Pixie Market, a store that caters to those who'd rather wear yellow shoes than black.

"My job allows me to travel the world and find all sorts of new designers, which is exciting," says Drevet. "But living in New York City has also been a huge influence on my style. It's made me want to be bolder." Currently, that style is a little more inspired by menswear from the '20s, but with a slim French silhouette. She wears black or gray straight-leg jeans, a white T-shirt, a men's-cut blazer, and silver derby flats most days.

Drevet's playful sense of style really comes out at night. "Dressing up at night is an art form for me. I like to have fun with it." Accessories include colorful resin '80s pieces, giant bow pins, chain headbands—the more creative, the better. "They always make my outfit."

Gaelle's Favorites

Stores: Pixie Market, Tokyu Hands (Tokyo), Blondie Vintage by Spitalfields Market (London), Le Printemps (Paris)
Online stores: pixiemarket.com, eBay.com, ugly-home.com
Style icon: Without a doubt, Bianca Jagger in a white suit arriving inside Studio 54 on a white horse for her birthday
Movies that inspire my style: *The Thomas Crown Affair* with Steve McQueen and Faye Dunaway is American chic at its finest. I also like *Trainspotting*, *Blowup*, *Desperately Seeking Susan*, and the original *Charlie's Angels* TV series.
What I listen to while getting ready for a night out: House music or anything '80s, Stevie Wonder, Blondie
What's worth the investment: A well-tailored black blazer is timeless.
Must-have piece: A scarf— it ties a look together.

From Gaelle's Closet

1.
Red felt cloche hat
I love the fantasy-fun element of this. I wear it at night for parties.

2.
Multicolor silk sleeveless short jumpsuit
My closet is filled with about a thousand jumpsuits—instant outfit!

3.
Red one-shoulder asymmetrical dress with white print and black felt pony
A great party dress—edgy, girly, and rock-glam.

4.
Black, gray, brown, and cream double-breasted cape
Something bold like a cape personalizes my style.

5.
Black-and-white geometric plastic link necklace with leather strap

Very new wave, early '80s. I like statement jewelry like this. Just wearing this alone with basics makes it an outfit.

6.
Black-and-blue silk tux jacket with floral print and round lapels

I wear this with black or gray jeans and a white T-shirt.

7.
Hermès watch

For day I'm minimalist with my accessories and wear only this. Super-French and chic.

8.
Metallic bronze lace-up shoes with cutouts

I designed these! I like the mix of masculine and feminine. They're very '20s but still modern in shiny metallic leather with little cutouts.

> **"FASHION IS LIKE A FANTASY—**
> *it takes you away from your daily life, so you should try to embrace it."*

Gallery Hopping
batwing sweater + **ankle-tie pants** + spectator boots

Night Out
ruched halter + **ankle-tie pants** + gladiator heels

smart shopping

Start with the basics

Don't get intimidated. Begin by buying a pair of thin black leggings and a long-sleeved leotard, and try layering them under your regular clothes, playing with proportions to figure out what you like best.

Bring a visual reference

An image sums up this look better than any words. When you go shopping, take along a photograph or a page from a magazine that shows something you like so you don't have to describe pieces to salespeople.

Buy jewelry from unexpected sources

Museum stores are a reliable resource for unusual jewelry—including reproductions of surprisingly good quality.

Worth the investment

Black suit pieces in medium-weight fabric like gabardine are a smart choice because they work all year round.

Shop with a friend

It's really worth being obsessive about picking and choosing exactly what to buy. Be prepared to try on a bunch of menswear black pants until you find the ones that slouch just right. Have a friend come along when you're looking for that one unique and kind-of-crazy piece to get an honest second opinion.

arty slick
store guide

Blake: Understated but avant-garde is the enduring mood here: There's no sign outside, and the pieces on the racks are equal parts dramatic and somber, like gunmetal taffeta tunics by Marni and Balenciaga schoolboy jackets. Bonus: They stock more Dries Van Noten than anyone else in the country. **Chicago, IL, 312-202-0047**

A Détacher: Though the in-house collection may seem intimidating, its pieces are actually easy to wear and incredibly flattering—crepe tulip-shaped dresses, watercolor floral tops. The storefront itself is a study in inspired minimalism: A grid of 90,000 tiny mirrors paves one wall, while the rest of the space is the palest lavender. **New York, NY, 212-625-3380**

Aloha Rag: For years, Honolulu-based Aloha Rag and its website have been the insider's secret source when one was on the lookout for that sold-out or seriously wait-listed Chloé bag or Ksubi jacket, but it is also justifiably beloved for its well-edited stock of labels like Commuun, and the best and newest jeans lines. And now, Aloha Rag is no longer a secret: Owner Tatsugo Yoda set up shop in spring 2008 in New York. **Honolulu, HI, 808-589-2050, and New York, NY, 212-925-0882, aloharag.com**

IF: SoHo's earliest retail pioneer (they opened a West Broadway location in 1979), IF has been similarly ahead of the curve when it comes to discovering and tracking the careers of the stars and the upstarts of the avant-garde. Look for everyone from Anne Demeulemeester to Japanese newcomers Tao and Toga. **New York, NY, 212-334-4964**

Kirna Zabête: When Beth Buccini and Sarah Easley opened their ultra-modern, emerging-label boutique in SoHo a decade ago, they offered a bold change of pace from the juggernaut of chains that had come to define the neighborhood's retail landscape. They continue to showcase designers they're passionate about: an unusually vibrant mix of Azzedine Alaïa, Rick Owens, and Proenza Schouler. **New York, NY, 212-941-9656, and Tokyo, Japan, 81-3-3356-6142, kirnazabete.com**

Linda Dresner: Highly conceptual labels for people who like to think—Junya Watanabe, Jil Sander, Undercover—are just a few of the lines arranged throughout these fittingly gallery-inspired spaces. **Birmingham, MI, 248-642-4999, and New York, NY, 212-308-3177, lindadresner.com**

Maison Martin Margiela: One of the poster children for deconstructed, challenging clothing, Martin Margiela focuses on expertly and often unexpectedly tailored pieces in a monochromatic palette. **maisonmartinmargiela.com for locations**

Maxfield: Situated in a bunker-like concrete building, this destination was the first on the West Coast to carry designers like Yohji Yamamoto and Comme des Garçons. Maxfield Bleu is its corresponding outlet, where an equally upscale vibe belies the discounted price tags. **Los Angeles, CA, 310-274-8800**

Hejfina: When Heiji Choy Black opened her iconoclastic store back in 2004, there was nothing like it in town. She took a chance on esoteric, then-unknown lines, and her indie-centric focus has not wavered. **Chicago, IL, 773-772-0002, hejfina.com**

Erie Basin: When you walk through the door of this exquisitely curated jewelry shop in the not-quite-gentrified Brooklyn neighborhood of Red Hook, it's like you've stepped 200 years into the past, to a sort of early America gone goth. We love the scarab pendants by Paul DeBlassie IV and bags by Natalia Brilli. **Brooklyn, NY, 718-554-6147, eriebasin.com**

Opening Ceremony: The emphasis here is on serious variety, as Opening Ceremony features the most forward-thinking, promising new labels from a particular city or country, each in yearlong increments (Hong Kong, London, and Brazil have been spotlighted in the past). The idea isn't the only thing that's conceptual—highlighted lines are always the most innovative that each city has to offer. **New York, NY, 212-219-2688, and Los Angeles, CA, 310-652-1120 openingceremony.us**

Ten Thousand Things: All but hidden in the increasingly hectic Meattpacking District, Ten Thousand Things is a source not only for the eponymous house line (a hardcore *Lucky* favorite—look for crave-worthy items like hammered silver discs that look like stacked shells) but also for Cara Croninger's iconic carved bangles, beads, and necklaces. **New York, NY, 212-352-1333**

bohemian

"My inspiration comes first from nature and then from artists like Andy Warhol, or even MTV," says Jade Jagger about her decadent, barefoot-on-the-beach style. That eclectic, high-low mesh of earthy and flashy is key to the Bohemian look. It's all about wearing rich pieces capriciously— frayed jeans and ornate jewelry, rough-hewn sandals with a delicate dress. Jane Birkin is the perfect icon, whether on the beach in Cannes, comfortable in a white tank, or on her wedding day in 1971, wearing a simple crochet slipdress. Decades later, the effect is still sophisticated and amazingly cool.

This page: Jane Birkin, 1975. Opposite, clockwise from top left: Nancy Wilson, 1978; Jade Jagger, 2004; Talitha and J. Paul Getty Jr. 1970; Stevie Nicks, 1970; Ali MacGraw, 1971; Lou Doillon, 2005.

bohemian
essential pieces

shrunken shearling jacket

skinny brown blazer

belted suede jacket

white trousers

'70s-style bell-bottoms

flared tweed trousers

drawstring-
waisted top

washed-silk
peasant blouse

blousy cropped
cardigan

beaded moroccan bolero

crochet-knit vest

furry vest

crinkled-silk tiered skirt

bright peasant skirt

fun ethnic-print skirt

bohemian
essential pieces

dip-dyed tank

button-down
prairie camisole

ruched empire-waist
tank

low-rise cords

floor-length skirt

patch-pocket jeans

flutter-sleeved chiffon dress

floral-print tunic dress

oversize wrap cardigan

long jersey dress

strappy wrap dress

maxi coat

bohemian
essential accessories

crochet heels

flat leather sandals

shearling ankle boots

hand-tooled leather
messenger bag

slouchy velvet
evening bag

ethnic-fabric hobo

glass and silver
teardrop earrings

feather and gold
earrings

matte gold and
diamond studs

layered beaded necklace

coin necklace

gold and diamond
snake ring

oversize
organic-stone ring

feather bracelet

hammered silver cuff

gold bangles

bohemian
how to get the look

FIT AND STYLING:
The Perfect Tunic

This Bohemian essential is a great casual-cool addition to any wadrobe. Most tunics are cut to be loose, but that doesn't mean baggy and unflattering. Just look for the following details:

- **A fitted shoulder and** three-quarter-length sleeves.

- **Slits at the sides—the fabric** should be ultra-thin, even sheer.

- **Anything goes when it comes** to color or pattern—from plain white to rainbow-colored paisley.

KEY ACCESSORY:
Gold Jewelry

Something that elevates this look to luxe hippie is the quality of your gold jewelry. You want it to be a deep, rich yellow tone, and you only get that from 20 karat gold or higher. (Many stores stock high-karat gold-plated pieces that can look just as good as the real thing.) We love the look of a 22 karat piece that's interspersed with colorful beads or raw-looking, unfinished diamonds, which are classic in an offhand way and have become much easier to find in recent years.

Bohemian Jeans

These should be made of soft, thin denim, and look like they were bought at a vintage store (even if they're brand new). Make sure they're fitted through the waist, hips, rear, and thighs; wide in the legs; and long enough to wear with your favorite platform boots.

The Statement Coat

With all the loose and flowy items that are key components of this look, having a few contrasting clean-lined pieces like a sharp brown blazer or fitted princess coat in the mix is essential for a vibe that's chic and not too artsy-hippie. A tailored black jacket worn over a long chiffon dress adds a touch of the unexpected (a key element of the Bohemian charisma). For daytime, a princess coat—knee-length or longer, double-breasted, military style—over short skirts, tall boots, or with maxi dresses just couldn't be cooler.

The Right Wrap Sweater

This is a cozy layering piece that is surprisingly sexy and so versatile. It looks equally great with a skinny tank and flared jeans as it does over a floral, hippie-girl dress, tights, and clunky boots. The key is to find one that's long—mid-thigh—and more drapey than chunky, so it echoes the sexy, carefree lines that make up most of the Boho wardrobe.

how to get the look

Looking Great in a Tiered Skirt

The fabric should be filmy and light, like a petticoat. The first tier should hit just below the hips—any higher and you run the risk of looking frumpy, as well as a good bit larger than your actual size. Make sure the waistline sits a few inches lower than your waist; otherwise, things start to look quite *Little House on the Prairie*.

Make a Statement with a Soft, Thin Scarf

This isn't about being practical. Don't tie the scarf, just sort of languidly wrap it once around your neck. And pair it with your barest camisoles. Look for scarves with a slow, fading ombre dye; fringed scarves in soft cotton; or ones with muted ethnic patterns. The scarf can be skinny or wide, but the fabric should be really thin, like silk or a cobwebby cashmere.

Layer a Furry Vest Under an Army Parka

This might not sound like the most natural combination, but it makes your slouchy-cool army parka look like it has taken on a glamorous new life. Look for a fitted fur (or fake fur) vest that is thin in texture. The shape should be slightly long and fluid, not at all boxy.

The Peasant Top

The peasant top can be deeply glamorous.
It should drape easily over your chest to
expose maximum collarbone, but not dip
into cleavage territory. Choose one with
elasticized long sleeves that you can
push up to the elbow, to give an
overall sense of the sultry
and undone.

bohemian
Lucky Girl
Liz McClean

OCCUPATION: Stylist/Fashion Designer
LOCATION: Brooklyn, NY

"I think of myself as a minimalist bohemian," says Brooklyn-based fashion designer and stylist Liz McClean. "I like anything nostalgic, anything that seems like it came from a time period before my own—drop-waists, puffed sleeves, lots of chiffon."

McClean tends to stick to a uniform of Empire-waist chiffon dresses, leggings, flat riding boots, and sweeping coats in the winter; gladiator sandals, lace camisoles, and baby-doll dresses for summer. "Once I put something together that I like, I pretty much wear it all the time," she says.

The minimalist element to her style comes from her super-spare color palette: She mostly wears black, navy, and dark wine. But that doesn't mean she's immune to a little ornamentation: "I have a thing about any kind of sparkle—my eye just jumps right to it," she says. "So I started collecting long, vintagey pendant necklaces from the '20s and '30s that feel nice to throw on for night, when I want a little glitter on me."

Liz's Favorites

Stores: The Holiday House, Barneys New York, Some Odd Rubies

Style eras: The '20s and '70s

Movies that inspire my style: *Immortal Beloved* is terribly romantic. There's a scene where a woman is bathing in a tub in this full-length bathing gown, and it's so sexy and beautiful. *The Virgin Suicides* is so, so dreamy. I also like *Grey Gardens*, *Taxi Driver*, and *Eyes of Laura Mars*.

What I listen to while getting ready for a night out: Anything by the Pixies

What's worth the investment: Because I live in New York, a good pair of flat knee-high boots and a winter coat.

Signature scents: Eau d'Hadrien by Annick Goutal, Mimosa by Calypso Christiane Celle

From Liz's Closet

1.
Black and cream chiffon dresses
I literally wear these day and night, every season. Sometimes when I want to be really casual, I'll throw a vintage T-shirt over this dress. I like that little bit of chiffon peeking out from underneath a worn tee.

2.
Vintage jean jacket
My favorite thing in the world is my sister Debbie's denim jacket from the '70s, which she bought when she was 13. We share custody of it. I guess it was once dark blue, but it's been washed and worn and repaired a million times, so now it's quite pale and super-soft.

3.
Vintage rhinestone necklace
I found this necklace at a vintage store in Brooklyn called Fluke years ago, and I wear it with just about anything when I need a little sparkle in my day.

4.
Giuseppe Zanotti Design gladiator sandals

I like that these are in a wine color, which is softer than black for summer, but still dark. I wear them with black leggings, a baby-doll chiffon dress, and my jean jacket.

5.
Vivienne Westwood coat

The big sculptural collar buttons up around the neck, so it looks interesting but still simple. It makes me feel like an urban warrior, kind of tough and dramatic.

6.
Chloé wedges

I have to be able to run around in all my shoes; otherwise I'll never wear them. These Chloé wedges are so incredibly comfortable and give me a little height.

"When it comes to getting myself dressed, I WANT TO LOOK UNIQUE, but I don't want to have to think about it too hard."

putting it together

A dip-dyed tank and cords look pulled together when paired with a leather bag and sandals.

An ethnic-fabric hobo and high-heeled sandals make this long jersey dress perfect for daytime.

Bell-bottoms, a prairie camisole, and leather wedges are effortless and cool.

A strappy wrap dress paired with metallic heels is simply sexy.

When the white trousers are slim, a peasant top and sling-backs look surprisingly dressy.

Balance a floor-length skirt with luxe items like an empire-waist tank and embellished flip-flops.

**peasant
dress**

winter

Pair it with a sweeping coat, brown leggings, and tall boots for a pulled-together look.

spring

To dress it up for spring, a little vest, wood-sole heels, and a slouchy bag add a dose of fun.

summer

Just a few strategic accessories—refined sandals, a silver cuff, a not-too-casual tote—are all you need to glam it up for summer evenings.

fall

In scaled-down, less-is-more proportions, rough-cozy leather pieces like a shearling jacket, ankle boots, and a satchel play up the mood without overpowering it.

bohemian
Lucky Girl

Liz Carey

OCCUPATION: Handbag Designer
LOCATION: Malibu, CA

Growing up in suburban Ohio in the acid-wash '80s, handbag designer Liz Carey had a dream: "I wanted to dress like a hippie and live by the beach," she says. But life, as they say, had other plans: At age 17 she became a model and, as models sometimes do, she married a rock star (Oasis' former drummer Alan White) and spent much of her twenties in London.

Now, at last, she has made her way to Malibu, where she lives with her current husband, actor Jake Weber, and their son, Waylon, and designs her line of luxe, earthy handbags in her sun-drenched backyard studio. "For the most part, my clothes are simple," she says. "I love my old Wrangler denim jacket and vintage camisoles."

When she does black-tie, Carey goes for floor-sweeping maxi dresses or knit minidresses. But dressed up or down, her faded, off-the-cuff glamour hinges on one special, defining touch: "I love, love, love my jewelry," Carey says. She wears precious metals and stones spun into organic, slinky snakes, lighthearted birds, and ethnic cuffs—anything unconventional-looking. "I wear it all, always," she says. "I sleep in my jewelry—that's luxury to me. That's bohemian."

Liz's Favorites

Stores: Rozark (for jewelry);
Planet Blue (for crochet dresses
and lingerie); Lost & Found
(for my favorite Épice scarves);
Hidden Treasures (for vintage
sundresses)
Style era: The '70s
Style icon: Jean Shrimpton
Movie that inspires my style:
Valley of the Dolls
**What I listen to while getting
ready for a night out:** Anything
by the Pretenders
Signature scents: Fracas by
Robert Piguet or patchouli oil
Vacation spot: Marbella, Spain

From Liz's Closet

1.
Silk sarong
I bought this in Thailand about 10 years ago—I wear it as a scarf, as a dress, and as a sarong.

2.
Temperley blue silk blouse
This is so elegant, and it looks amazing with jeans.

3.
Snake cuff bracelets
One of these was a present from my friend after I had my son, and the other one my husband gave me. When I wear them, they remind me of my fellas.

4.
Purple crochet bathing suit
I found this at Planet Blue in Malibu. I thought I would never wear it, but strangely enough, it looks great on. It kind of covers your belly where you want it to but lets some sexy parts show. And the color is amazing.

"I grew up in Ohio, where there was amazing vintage stuff. When I was 16, **I FOUND AN OLD OSSIE CLARK DRESS FROM THE '60S,** which was so special and unique—it really turned me onto the style of that whole era."

5.
**Bird Handbags
Guatemalan fabric purse**
The colors on this are so vibrant—
I made it from shirts I picked up
in Guatemala. I liked the fabric so
much, I ended up keeping some of
the shirts for myself.

6.
**Vintage gauze
rainbow dress**
I bought this a couple of
summers ago for maybe $5 in
Venice Beach. My friends are
always borrowing it from me.
It's beautiful and summery.

7.
Levi's denim miniskirt
I *live* in this skirt. It is so
comfortable.

8.
**Bird Handbags metallic
sea blue corset clutch**
This is a handbag from my
collection. The sea blue color is
unusual and special.

9.
**Manolo Blahnik green
lizard heels**
I bought these as a present for
myself on my 28th birthday, and
they are my favorite color. They
are proof that if you spend a lot of
money on shoes, they will last.

one piece, two ways

Weekend Party
cinched-waist top + **red peasant skirt** + t-strap sandals

Morning Errands
peasant top + **red peasant skirt** + embellished flats

bohemian
smart shopping

Look for thin material

Camisoles are the base layer for almost every Bohemian outfit, so look for ones made out of silk, not cotton—which can stick and cling to other materials. The idea is that when you throw on a sheer peasant top, it will glide over what's underneath.

Worth the investment

Go for a 100 percent pashmina scarf over a silk-pashmina blend. It's so much softer and more luxurious.

Wooden heels, please

Always buy high-heeled boots with stacked wooden heels. Leather-covered heels shred easily if worn every day.

Go straight to the source

Jewelry, silk tunics, camisoles, and moccasins are gorgeous and inexpensive bought directly from stores offering Indian imports.

Dye it yourself

If you find a piece you adore—say a great peasant top that fits perfectly— but it's in a way-too-bright pattern, buy it anyway and dye it another, deeper color. You'll make a loud pattern more subtle *and* give it a unique, hand-dipped quality.

bohemian
store guide

Dosa: Defined by a soothingly neutral palette, the upscale offerings here, which include washed-silk skirts and finely woven sweaters, are all intended to be layered, but work beautifully on their own as well. **New York, NY, 212-431-1733, and Los Angeles, CA, 213-489-2801, dosainc.com**

Fabindia.com: Using soft handwoven cotton that's printed with traditional techniques and vegetable dyes, this site specializes in the most gorgeous, affordable, beach-perfect caftans direct from New Delhi.

Govinda's Imports: Located next to a Hare Krishna temple, this shop—much beloved by stylists—is the go-to spot in L.A. for affordable, traditional Indian chandelier earrings, silk tunics, and printed cotton sarongs. **Los Angeles, CA, 310-204-3263, govindasimports.com**

Gypsymoon.com: A *Faeirie Queene* aesthetic predominates at this Boston-based Web enterprise. In addition to a house line of washed silk and velvet patchwork silks, the site peddles loads of difficult-to-find Bohemian-tinged labels, like Rozae Nichols, Gary Graham, and Chan Luu.

Layla: Tucked away off Brooklyn's Atlantic Avenue, this pleasingly minimal little store stocks exquisite Indian jewelry and silk bedding. They carry their own line of exquisitely cut block-printed slipdresses and kurtas, along with a few selects from designers like Virginia Johnson and Erica Tanov. **Brooklyn, NY, 718-222-1933, layla-bklyn.com**

Matta: Known for its cotton sarongs and printed silk textiles, Matta, housed in an airy sliver of a space, can winterize for an East Coast version of Boho style come cold weather: Look for its own cashmere tunics and swingy tops, which mingle with Aoyama Itchome dresses, A Common Thread sweaters, patterned socks, carryalls, and Isabel Marant blouses. **New York, NY, 212-343-9399, mattany.com**

Miguelina: Originally famous for its stock of lace-trimmed silk tops, Miguelina's all-white West Village flagship brims with colorful vacation wear that has a distinctly tropical edge. Look for tangerine-hued tunics, crochet-festooned dresses, and paisley-printed cover-ups. **New York, NY, 212-400-3100, miguelina.com**

Salt: This calming, ultra-minimal spot has the feel of a luxe yoga studio, and draws less-is-more loyalists in search of bohemian-around-the-edges pieces: There is a range of subdued, monochromatic hits, like printed scarves, sweaters by The Avant, and stackable fire opal rings from Melissa Joy Manning. **Los Angeles, CA, 310-452-1154**

Uzbekalive.com: A secret resource for beautiful, bright silk ikat scarves in a range of colors and patterns—few of which top $50, and most of which cost much less.

Vajra Pema: Pema Yangzom's store is brimming with authentic Indian jewelry. There are tons of styles in a variety materials from sterling silver to 22 karat gold—and a constant, rotating supply of 100 percent pashmina scarves, leather sandals, and tiny beaded purses. **New York, NY, 212-529-4344, vajrapema.com**

Robin Richman: Former knitwear designer Robin Richman's shop has an appealing industrial-folkloric mood: Gauzy hand-dyed Gary Graham dresses rest on antique wrought-iron racks and chunky bead necklaces drape from vintage glass knobs. **Chicago, IL, 773-278-6150, robinrichman.com**

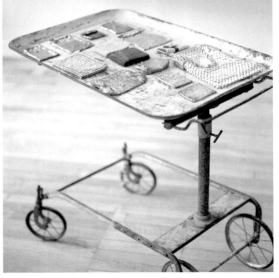

Erica Tanov: A wispy femininity permeates all of San Francisco–based Tanov's peasant tops, dresses, and bed jackets. You'll also find a careful edit of pieces by other names—Megan Park, Kerry Cassill—filling out the racks at her antique-filled shops. **San Francisco, CA, 415-674-1228, and New York, NY, 212-334-8020, ericatanov.com**

New York Adorned: Exotic jewelry, including owner Lori Leven's exquisitely crafted pieces, abounds at this tattoo parlor/piercing studio. **New York, NY, 212-473-0007, nyadorned.com**

Roberta Freymann: Meander through this color-drenched shop—part of a growing mini empire—and find breezy, Indian-influenced clothing; richly adorned garments Freymann picks up on her global treks; and heaps of vibrant bedding. **New York, NY, 212-585-3767, roberta-freymann.com**

gamine

Just like Audrey Hepburn's character in *Sabrina*, a schoolgirl who travels overseas and returns transformed, Gamine is an intercontinental mix of clean American lines and French insouciance. It's about the perfect striped shirt and what makes a trench coat cute, instead of unfeminine. The wardrobe couldn't be more simple or timeless—cotton cardigans; cool, lovely floral dresses; old-school espadrilles; boatneck sweaters in navy and red—but it's put together in an offhand, pedaling-to-the-market kind of way. This girl-sophisticate feel comes from playing with expectations and keeping things mysterious thanks to an innate knack for balance. Take director Sofia Coppola, who famously wore ballet flats to the Oscars. Or reigning Gamine Charlotte Gainsbourg, who always has simple hair and makeup, and whose shoes and bag never quite go with the rest of her outfit, but who for our money is the best-dressed girl in Paris.

This page: Audrey Tatou, 2005. Opposite page, clockwise from top left: Charlotte Gainsbourg, 2007; Kirsten Dunst, 2007; Audrey Hepburn, 1960; Jean Seberg, 1959; Sofia Coppola, 2004; Julie Delpy, 2002.

boxy lace silk blouse

thin-knit red t-shirt

black scoopneck t-shirt

belted safari dress

floral tie-neck dress

lacy baby-doll dress

striped boatneck top

classic crewneck t-shirt

quirky patterned top

striped cotton
cardigan

short-sleeved
dolman sweater

striped buttoned
turtleneck

flared sailor skirt

silk tie-waist skirt

bubble miniskirt

gamine
essential pieces

double-breasted cardigan   indigo smock jacket   bright cropped jacket

raw denim skinny jeans   wide-leg trousers   parachute silk cargo pants

nautical tank top

oversize chambray
button-down shirt

brown leather
biker jacket

pedal pushers

tailored trench coat

belted cotton tunic

gamine
essential accessories

patent leather
sandals

ankle-strap
black flats

slingback wedge
sandals

ankle-tie espadrilles

cork-heel platform sandals

skinny red belt

basic brown leather belt

brown wedge boots

stainless steel
diver's watch

dainty charm
necklace

alligator cuff

duffel-style handbag

striped knit hat

fancy quilted purse
with chain strap

cotton and rope satchel

black scarf

how to get the look

FIT AND STYLING:
The Perfect Floral Dress

This is all about the balance of sweetly pretty and grown-up. Look for the following details:

- **A shape that's sleek and well-cut in cotton or silk.**

- **Prints in shades like red, fuchsia, navy, and yellow.** But sheer watercolor shades look beautiful on diaphanous fabrics too.

- **Pattern is very important:** A tiny, uniform print (rather than an abstract one of varying size, shape, and color) is genuinely Gamine—sweet and sophisticated at the same time.

- **Lovely touches like a small ruffle at the waist or sleeve are nice**—but pass on any extras like bows or pleats. The actual design should be clearly meant for a woman—not a girl.

Complete the Look with a Graphic Scarf

This instant add-on cuts the too-cute factor that can happen with this look. Choose a bold pattern, like a black-and-white check. Think your dress is a bit twee? Throw a scarf on. Your tank and pedal pushers lacking edge? This will take care of that in seconds.

Gamine Jeans

What makes these right is how they seem unique to the girl wearing them—they start out dark, untreated, and stiff (A.P.C. makes the all-time best ones in shapes for every body type), and then over time, fade and form to the body in the most perfect way. The constants are a mid-to-high waistline that's neither trendy nor traditional and a slender, clean, stovepipe leg.

The Right Boatneck T-shirt

Choose one with three-quarter-length sleeves, a hemline that hits past the hips, and an extra-wide neckline in shades like navy, red, or gray. Fancy or sporty, it's a T-shirt at the end of the day, so feel free to be flexible in terms of styling.

Stick with a Classic Peacoat

The cut of this sailor-boy-influenced staple is simple and nautical—single- or double-breasted, an A-line silhouette, and a hem that hits just past the hip (though cropped versions can be fun too). We like it best in navy—like true sailors wear—but red, black, and camel are great as well.

how to get the look

Look Authentic in a Sailor-Stripe Shirt

When it comes to this top, we take our styling cues from Jean Seberg in *Breathless*: thin stripes in red and white or navy and white, with long sleeves that you can push up, and a boat or crew neckline. What's key to the look is that the fit is not tight, but just a little slouchy.

MUST-HAVE SHOE:
Espadrilles

Totally beachy, totally Cannes circa 1962, these can be sexy or casual, depending on the height of the heel you choose and the outfit you pair them with. We like espadrilles in all sorts of fabrics—like canvas, suede, or even silk—as well as colors, and we like to wear them laced—not up the leg, but secured around the ankle.

ICONIC ITEM:
The Trench Coat

Volumes have been written about the timeless, chic power of the trench. It's that essential. But it's easy to tread into the private-detective zone if you don't get a few things right—namely, a generous collar and skinny arm. Think clean and unfussy, light and fancy. Choose one in classic beige, and, if possible, with a removable lining that you can take out when it's warm. The length should be mid-thigh or longer. And always knot the belt. That's the Charlotte Gainsbourg trench, and that's what we want, too.

gamine
Lucky Girl
Roanne Adams

OCCUPATION: Designer/Art Director
LOCATION: New York, NY

When you look at the individual elements—blazers, '70s-inspired sundresses, and boat shoes—it seems like Roanne Adams' wardrobe is preppy, rather than Gamine. But when the art director puts it all together, her outfits seem to always work in that indefinably perfect way. "I never wear anything too over-the-top girly," she says. "And if I do I pair it with my riding boots."

A lot of her sense of style, she says, evolved as a result of living in France for four years during her teens. "I moved to Paris in seventh grade, and then came back to Connecticut for my senior year. It was confusing because everyone in my high school wore sweatpants, and I was used to wearing little skirts and vintage fur coats to class." When she moved to New York after graduation, her style took a more professional turn.

These days, Adams likes feminine-cut blouses that have an edge to them, or black silk trousers with a high waist and straight legs. She likes to wear vintage scarves to add a bit of drama. "I'm fairly casual," she says. "But I like to wear slightly left-of-center pieces."

Roanne's Favorites

Stores: Steven Alan, Mick Margo, Oak, Earnest Sewn, vintage stores (the farther from Manhattan, the better)
Online store: refinery29shops.com
Style icons: Jane Birkin and Charlotte Gainsbourg
Movie that inspires my style: Faye Dunaway in *Bonnie and Clyde*
What I listen to while getting ready for a night out: Fleetwood Mac's *Rumours*
What's worth the investment: A Chanel purse and a Burberry trench coat
Signature scent: Philosykos eau de toilette by Diptyque

From Roanne's Closet

1.
Opening Ceremony black-and-white silk A-line tank dress
This is just incredibly comfortable. The pattern appeals to my graphic sensibilities. I wear this on the hottest New York summer days. I sometimes put spandex shorts on underneath to make it bike-friendly!

2.
Black pony-skin flats
Super-cute, and I can zip around on my bike all day in them.

3.
White leather clutch
I couldn't handle carrying around a big bag at night—I would stress about what to put in it. This clutch is so simple and bold. I just throw in some money and a lipstick, and it is a nice accent to all my outfits.

4.
Black suede ankle boots
I've had these for years. They are the best pair of heels I've ever purchased. They make me look tall, and they're incredibly comfortable. And there's something about the platform stiletto heel that drastically improves my dance moves! I typically wear these with skinny jeans or opaque black stockings and a smock dress.

5.

BCBG white silk sleeveless dress with ruffled neck
I bought this dress at the last minute for a New Year's Eve White Party, and it turned out to be just right.

6.

Diamond art deco bracelet
I wear this on special occasions. It pairs nicely with dresses like my BCBG sleeveless one because of its *Great Gatsby*–roaring '20s feel, which is one of my favorite dressy looks.

7.

3.1 Phillip Lim beige silk blouse
This is such a beautiful blouse—the colors, the combination of fabrics, the pattern. I wear it several ways, but it looks best dressed up, tucked into a high-waisted black pencil skirt with pumps and a blazer.

8.

Rhinestone starburst pendant
This belonged to my grandmother. It's the perfect amount of ornamentation since I tend to wear solid colors without much flair.

9.

Vena Cava black wide-leg pants
I've had these for a while—I just can't imagine what I would do without them. I love to tuck blouses into them.

"I live in Tribeca and I bike to work every day. Occasionally, I'll get dressed up and bike somewhere at night, but never in super-high heels."

putting it together

Ballet flats are ideal for keeping a tie-neck dress and quilted purse looking casual.

Balance wide-leg trousers with a nautical tank top and unfussy white sandals.

Wedge espadrilles with skinny jeans create a long, flattering line.

Show off the cool waistline of a silk tie-waist skirt by tucking in a patterned tee.

Pair a flirty miniskirt with a utilitarian top, such as this oversize chambray button-down.

Red-on-red looks great when done casually with peep-toe wedges and a cropped jacket.

thin
military
pants

winter

These pants couldn't be more utilitarian-chic with a blousy sweater, a hooded coat, and flat ankle boots.

spring

Pair with a tiny cardigan, a timeless trench, and ballerina flats for a stylish alternative to jeans.

summer

The pants are simple enough for daytime with a slightly punky tee, bright wedges, and a bucket bag.

fall

For an instant Parisian-girl look, simply add a sexy sweater, belted jacket, and polished purse.

gamine
Lucky Girl
Emma Fletcher

OCCUPATION: Clothing Designer
LOCATION: New York, NY

"I'm in this phase right now where I want to be Amish—I like the
purity of that look," says Emma Fletcher. "I love high-quality,
beautiful pieces that are dressed down, everything nice and simple."
Her clothing line, Lyell—with boutiques in Paris and Manhattan—
has become the go-to brand for women in search of perfectly cut silk
blouses and dresses, and her own look is the embodiment of elegant,
enigmatic, Gamine cool. "I get a lot of my inspiration from movies,
photos, and vintage clothing; usually something catches my eye and
I'll build from there," she says.

Fletcher gravitates toward silhouettes from the '30s and
'70s—when "things were very boyish and feminine at the same
time"—lines that are slim and straight, fabrics that are fine
and silky, details that are delicate.

Yet despite all the fragility, Fletcher is refreshingly practical and
utilitarian about what she needs back from her wardrobe. "Honestly,
I wear my clothes, and I walk in my shoes. Yes, everything needs
to be beautiful and tailored, but it also needs to be something I can
wear day in and day out."

Emma's Favorites

Stores: A.P.C., A Détacher, Mayle
Style icon: Charlotte Rampling is my favorite: her eyes, her hair, her face, her body.
Movies that inspire my style: *Don't Look Now, Three*
What's worth the investment: Handbags or shoes. I am rough on shoes, though, so more likely I'll spend my money on a handbag.
I can't live without: My mum's knitted scarf
Colors: Black and cream
Shoes: Vintage Ferragamos with a round toe

From Emma's Closet

1.
Lyell V-pleat black dress
It doesn't need any accessorizing—just tights and flats.

2.
Lyell black silk jacket
I think this is so versatile. It's easy to wear, whether you tie the belt tightly or wear it loosely tied at the back. And the ivory silk lining feels amazing.

3.
Vintage white sleeveless top
My friend Maria gave me this top. She lives in Paris and owns Marie Louise De Monterey, which shares space with the Lyell Paris store. She carries vintage and baby vintage clothing—very beautiful antique pieces.

4.
Vintage bird pin
I had an old pin with two birds kissing that broke in two, and I was heartbroken over it. So my friend, the jewelry designer Derrick Cruz, carved a similar one and we molded a collection of them to sell at the Lyell store.

5.
Vintage Ferragamo boots
I collect these for the store. They are a perfect midnight blue. I wear them with wide-leg jeans.

6.
Lyell white knit vest
The vest is made of baby alpaca. The yoke is macrame and the rest is handknit. I throw it over any outfit, and it is warm and cozy without being bulky. Definitely a unique piece.

7.
Vintage velvet floral-print jacket
I like this jacket because it is so old, yet on account of the bold print, it has a modern feel. It looks great over dresses or just with jeans and a camisole.

8.
Lyell black Poppy skirt
This is a basic English wool crepe skirt with a silk art deco–print lining. I love it because it can be worn with any blouse.

9.
Mayle brown leather handbag
I never carried a bag before this one. It's the perfect length, color, size—everything. It's simple, and I love that it doesn't have a million unnecessary zips, tassels, and pockets.

"I love silk pieces—silk chiffon, silk velvet—with **LITTLE BITS OF LACE** or tiny pleating or embroidery to them."

gamine
one piece, two ways

Low-Key Date
shoulder-tie cami + dark jeans + strappy gold sandals

Summer Barbecue
shoulder-tie cami + bubble skirt + wedge espadrilles

smart shopping

Customize the fit of your denim

For those with an absolute—and we do mean absolute—commitment to breaking in raw denim for that perfect, faded-along-the-hip look: Soak in a bathtub wearing your new jeans, and then let them dry and mold to your body. Also, wash them inside out, and always air-dry them.

Consider synthetics

We love floral dresses in silk and chiffon, but we also adore floral dresses in a poly-blend (like those made by French designer and long-time queen of Gamine, Agnès B.). The fabric is as thin as silk and drapes beautifully.

Buy secondhand

Silk scarves—even designer ones—are easy to find in thrift stores, on eBay, and in flea markets. Nothing beats the insouciant glamour of a really fantastic scarf from one of the greats like Chanel knotted sweetly around the neck.

Do a quality check

Take a close look at the shoulder seams on your sailor shirt and make sure the stripes line up. If they're not uniform, it's a sure sign the top is badly made.

Go straight to the source

Search out authentic pieces in an army-navy store for sailor shirts, espadrilles, sailcloth smocks, and peacoats that are a bit rugged and genuine in feel.

gamine
store guide

Addiction: Proprietress Nikki Salk is a poster child for a wilder and slightly more idiosyncratic version of Gamine style, and her shop is packed with what she herself wants to wear, from electric blue minidresses to simple tunics made from shirting material. **Atlanta, GA, 678-927-9383, shop-addiction.com**

A.P.C.: A must-visit: Expect a bounty of utilitarian pieces every season, including subtly pintucked tops, perfectly tailored trenches, and ribbon-trimmed sailor dresses. This is where the women who do this look exactly right get their building blocks. **New York, NY, 212-966-9685, and Paris, France, 33153634370, apc.fr**

Brittanyboutique.com: Paper-thin striped boating shirts, smocks cut from sailcloth, blue-and-white espadrilles, and bright yellow oilskin raincoats are hallmarks of this thoroughly Provence, bare-bones Web site.

Espadrillesetc.com: This stylist's secret weapon stocks one thing only: canvas espadrilles in everything from slate gray to sailor-inspired red-and-white stripes.

Lagarconne.com: Sharp graphics, featherweight fonts, and pages that look like sheets of slides on a light box are emblematic of this Web boutique. Click past the edgier picks to uncover simple Vena Cava dresses, Heimstone vests, and Repetto tap shoes.

London Sole: The best resource out there for ballet flats in any and every conceivable color and pattern. **londonsole.com for locations**

Lyell: Deftly mixing a tightly edited selection of vintage with her own line of masterfully tailored pieces, owner Emma Fletcher's Victorian-esque shop is a one-stop deal for loading up on refined dresses and blouses. **New York, NY, 212-966-8484, and Paris, France, 33148048388, lyellnyc.com**

Isabel Marant: The French designer is revered for creating flattering, super-clean pieces that are just a touch bohemian around the edges. Marant has an intensely loyal following. **Paris, France, 33149237540, isabelmarant.tm.fr**

Ludivine: Classic Parisian labels like Les Prairies des Paris and Claudine Pierlot are evergreens at this carefully edited, very French boutique. Adorable Provence-born Ludivine Grégoire—who herself executes the look expertly—even selected the West Village location of her shop for its similarities to Paris' maze-like Third Arrondissement. **New York, NY, 646-336-6576, boutiqueludivine.com**

Steven Alan: Over the last two decades, Steven Alan has been a hugely influential force in New York City retailing, continually promoting a vibe that's sort of boyish and sort of girlish at the same time. Key piece: one of the perfectly rumpled button-downs from his eponymous line. **New York, NY, 212-343-0692, and Los Angeles, CA, 310-854-1814, stevenalan.com**

Vanessa Bruno: American fashion editors, who are obsessed with Bruno's modern, feminine designs, flock to her three Paris outposts whenever they are in town for the shows. To have access to her entire line in one place is a thrill; in the States, you're lucky to find just a few pieces here and there. **Paris, France, 33142614460, vanessabruno.com**

Zadig & Voltaire: Style-conscious French girls who have the uniform down pat swear by Zadig & Voltaire, which turns out just-a-tad-slouchy trousers and luxuriously thin cotton sweaters. Though based in Paris, they have a California outpost and an e-commerce site. **Paris, France, 33140709789, and Los Angeles, CA, 310-358-9616, zadig-et-voltaire.com**

mix+
match

Starring the *Lucky* Staffers

Naturally, most people can't be neatly categorized into a single iconic look. Personal style is a fun, ever-changing thing, and we are all about being creative and mixing it up a bit— some Posh Eclectic flash with a bit of American Classic neatness; Euro Chic layered with Mod. Here's some of the *Lucky* staff wearing their favorite combinations.

mix + *match*

Bohemian + American Classic

Ann Brady, Senior Associate Fashion Editor

"I like looking sharp, but in a low-key way. The blazer over the floaty tunic keeps the look sophisticated, and the riding boots are sexy but practical."

American Classic + Rock and Roll

Kathryn Irby, Accessories Market Assistant

"This shrunken bomber jacket and oversize tuxedo shirt paired with my short, flat boots is a favorite outfit. It's clean but still pretty tough."

mix+match

Euro Chic + Bombshell
Meredith Kahn Rollins, Executive Editor
"I wear classics like cardigans and pencil skirts, but
I like the fit to be a bit more curvy. It makes this
conservative outfit look just a bit seductive."

Bombshell + Rock and Roll
Regan A. Solmo, Managing Editor
"This jacket is classic Rock and Roll, but the muted
color softens the edge a bit, so it blends well with a
feminine bustier and sleek black capris."

Arty Slick + Rock and Roll
Melissa Lum, Accessories Editor
"I love the idea of a *Gigi*-style black dress, but with a little something extra. Over-the-knee boots, layered chain necklaces, and bangles complete the look."

Gamine + Mod
Natalie Benotti, Fashion Associate
"I am a huge vintage fan, and I love this mesh of two different '60s looks—sailor pants and a retro cardigan. The overall effect is very graphic and clean."

Rock and Roll + Posh Eclectic

Nicola Miller, Associate Fashion Editor

"On its own, this lace dress is ladylike and fancy. But when I contrast it with black tights and a vest, it suddenly takes on an edgier, thrift-store-glam feel."

Posh Eclectic + Gamine

Jenny Kang, Associate Market Editor

"I like the effect of pairing opposites together. This blazer is so tailored, and the skirt is so sweet, that by contrasting them, both pieces stand out even more."

Euro Chic + Mod
Julia Topolski, Accessories Director

"It's hard to go wrong wearing all-black. I like the '60s feel of this minidress, but the interesting shape makes it sophisticated."

Mod + American Classic
Bridget Buckley, Bookings Director

"I live in jeans and white button-downs. But when I want to look more chic, the pattern and retro cut of this '60s-style coat changes the whole silhouette."

mix+match

California Casual + Bombshell
Alexandra Willinger, Associate Fashion Editor
"I prefer a simple, polished look that's not too fancy.
Since this high-waisted pencil skirt is dressy, I keep
it low-key by tucking in my favorite plaid shirt."

Bombshell + Gamine
Lauren DeCarlo, Fashion News Editor
"It's sexy and unexpected to add a masculine item to
pretty outfits. I love wearing this chunky sailor-style
cardigan with a slipdress. And these boots are killer."

mix+*match*

Rock and Roll + Gamine
Cat Marnell, Beauty Assistant
"This outfit is totally Blondie-goes-to-Nantucket.
The trench and low-heeled ankle boots are elegant and
modest, so I can get away with skintight vinyl pants."

American Classic + Posh Eclectic
Emily McCarthy, Editorial Assistant
"I always like to feel put together, and dresses
are the ultimate ready-made outfit. I love the casual
jacket paired with fun, vintage-style T-strap heels."

exclusive deals, discounts & giveaways
lucky breaks

Offers are valid from October 1, 2008, through November 30, 2008, or while supplies last.
Discounts and prices do not include shipping or taxes.

BARNEYS NEW YORK CO-OP

The edgy, younger sibling of uptown fashion mecca Barneys New York carries an impressive selection of established and up-and-coming designers and beauty brands. Log on to www.luckymag.com/breaks to enter for a chance to win one of five $2,000 gift cards.

VENA CAVA
EMBROIDERED-
TOP DRESS
$550

VIRGINIA JOHNSON
WOOL SHAWL $210

FETTY
STERLING AND DIAMOND
BRAILLE BANGLES
$735 EACH

5
shopping sprees
worth **$2,000**
each

SHINE HARDCORE
LIP GLOSS IN
RED SINNER $22

LOEFFLER RANDALL
"YVETTE" BOOTIES $575

Madewell

Ingeniously simple and cool, the recently launched J. Crew offshoot specializes in easy cotton tops, sturdy leather bags, and slim-cut jeans. Log on to www.luckymag.com/breaks to enter for a chance to win one of five $2,000 gift cards.

"CELIE" PLEATED
SHELL TOP $98

BELTED LEATHER
BOMBER $495

GIANT LEATHER
PUFFY TOTE $298

5
shopping sprees
worth **$2,000**
each

Piperlime

One of our go-to resources for footwear online, this site has a vast list of designers—from Giuseppe Zanotti to Sam Edelman—at a wide range of prices. Log on to www.luckymag.com/breaks to enter for a chance to win one of twenty $500 gift cards.

20
shopping sprees
worth **$500**
each

SAM EDELMAN
"ISADOR" FLATS $80

ARTURO CHIANG
"TAMARA" ANKLE BOOTS $160

**14K GOLD "MONTAUK" DAISY BAND
WITH DIAMONDS** RETAIL VALUE $1,500

7
diamond rings
worth **$1,500**
each

HELEN FICALORA

We're longtime fans of this collection of super-delicate, nature-inspired jewelry, made with gold, silver, and gemstones. Log on to www.luckymag.com/breaks to enter for a chance to win one of seven rings worth $1,500 each.

Active Endeavors

This popular website carries an extensive roster of emerging and well-known labels, all organized in super-navigable categories for easy shopping. Log on to www.luckymag.com/breaks to enter for a chance to win one of ten $1,000 gift cards.

PLUS Log on to www.activeendeavors.com and enter "luckybreaks1" at checkout to save 25 percent. Sale items excluded.

10
shopping sprees
worth **$1,000**
each

plus

25% OFF

TIBI SCOOPNECK DRESS REGULARLY $390 **LUCKY BREAKS PRICE $292.50**

**MARNIE BUGS LEATHER
"AMELIA" CLUTCH** REGULARLY $341
LUCKY BREAKS PRICE $255.75

HOBO INTERNATIONAL

Well-made and well-designed, these minimalist purses, belts, and wallets come in tons of sleek styles and fun colors. Log on to www.hobobags.com and enter "luckybreaks4" at checkout to save 25 percent on everything.

25% OFF everything

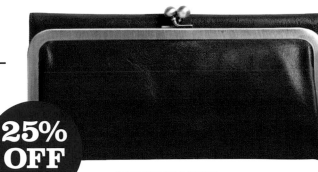

"RACHEL" CLUTCH WALLET
REGULARLY $118 **LUCKY BREAKS PRICE $88.50**

Shopbop

Not only does this mega online boutique stock more than 200 brands, it also offers a ton of outstanding designer exclusives. Log on to www.luckymag.com/breaks to enter for a chance to win one of two $5,000 gift cards.

2 shopping sprees worth **$5,000** each

OPENING CEREMONY
SUEDE HIGH-HEEL PUMPS $405

MARC BY
MARC JACOBS RESIN AND
METAL NECKLACE $78

BOP BASICS
POLYESTER SCOOP
TEE DRESS $180

urbanoutfitters.com

Always on-trend and well-priced, this beloved chain consistently turns out streetwise-chic clothing and accessories, as well as vintage-inspired home furnishings. Log on to www.urbanoutfitters.com and enter "luckybreaks8" at checkout to save 25 percent on everything.

CLASSIC EXTRA-LONG-SLEEVE T-SHIRT
REGULARLY $55 EACH
LUCKY BREAKS PRICE $41.25 EACH

**WOODSY
AGATE NECKLACE**
REGULARLY $34
**LUCKY BREAKS
PRICE $25.50**

25% OFF everything

**SILENCE & NOISE SMOCKED
TIE-BACK DRESS** REGULARLY $68
LUCKY BREAKS PRICE $51

LEATHER LACE RIDING BOOT
REGULARLY $150
LUCKY BREAKS PRICE $112.50

C&C CALIFORNIA

This line is known for laid-back-sexy, unbelievably soft, super-thin tees and dresses. Log on to www.candccalifornia.com and enter "luckybreaks9" at checkout to save 25 percent on everything.

25% OFF everything

Searle

Stocked with all things sophisticated, this store carries everything from drapey cashmere cardigans to black-tie gowns. Log on to www.luckymag.com/breaks to enter for a chance to win one of ten $1,000 gift cards.

10 shopping sprees worth **$1,000** each

LAUREN MERKIN "AVA" LAMBSKIN CLUTCH $298

MORRA DESIGNS BRUSHED GOLD DISC NECKLACE $128

BIBELOT CASHMERE GATHERED-FRONT CARDIGAN $358

The Body Shop

The bath and body products from this iconic brand are made with fair-trade ingredients and are super-affordable. Log on to www.thebodyshop.com and enter "luckybreaks5" at checkout to save 25 percent on everything.

25% OFF everything

CREAM EYE COLOR IN DUSK PINK
REGULARLY $12 **LUCKY BREAKS PRICE $9**

EYE COLOR IN PEACOCK GREEN
REGULARLY $12 **LUCKY BREAKS PRICE $9**

VITAMIN E MOISTURE CREAM
REGULARLY $16 **LUCKY BREAKS PRICE $12**

306

TOCCA

The romantic dresses and luxe fragrances from this gorgeous line are the definition of elegant bohemian. Log on to www.tocca.com and enter "luckybreaks6" at checkout to save 25 percent on everything. For every order, Tocca will donate $1 to breast cancer research.

25% OFF everything

STELLA EAU DE PARFUM
REGULARLY $68
LUCKY BREAKS PRICE $51

SILK "CONSTANCE" DRESS
REGULARLY $418
LUCKY BREAKS PRICE $313.50

Branch

An amazing line of jewelry based on organic shapes—branches, shells, rose petals—in high-karat gold and silver. Log on to www.branchjewelry.com and enter "luckybreaks2" at checkout to save 25 percent on everything. For every order, Branch will donate $1 to breast cancer research.

25% OFF everything

18K GOLD BLADE OF GRASS EARRINGS
REGULARLY $1,550
LUCKY BREAKS PRICE $1,162.50

18K GOLD TINY LEAF NECKLACE
REGULARLY $475
LUCKY BREAKS PRICE $356.25

18K GOLD SEED RING WITH DIAMOND
REGULARLY $600 **LUCKY BREAKS PRICE $450**

Hayden-Harnett

These lush leather and fabric handbags are understated, with just a bit of edge to them. Log on to www.haydenharnett.com and enter "luckybreaks3" at checkout to save 25 percent on everything. For every order, Hayden-Harnett will donate $1 to breast cancer research.

25% OFF everything

"EMILE" BOWLER TOTE
REGULARLY $560
LUCKY BREAKS PRICE $420

special thanks to the following designers, whose clothes and accessories were used in this book:

18th Amendment

A
Aerosoles
Aigle
Alexander Wang
Alexis Bittar
Alice + Olivia
American Apparel
Amo & Bretti
Amrita Singh
Anna Sui
Annelore
April, May
Autumn Cashmere

B
Balenciaga
Banana Republic
BCBG Max Azria
Belle by Sigerson Morrison
Bird Handbags
Birkenstock
Black Halo
Bliss Lau
Blumarine
BOSS Orange
Brooks Brothers
Built by Wendy
Burberry

C
C&C California
Cartier
Catherine Malandrino
Cesare Paciotti
Chanel
Charles Nolan
Charlotte Ronson
Chloé

Christian Louboutin
Christopher's
Claire's
Coach
Coclico
Converse
Cool Hunting People

D
Dana David
David Yurman
Davis by Ruthie Davis
Deborah Sweeney
Delman
Derek Lam
Diane von Furstenberg
DKNY
Dolce & Gabbana
Dries Van Noten

E
Earnest Sewn
Edun
Elizabeth Gillett
Elizabeth Yarborough
Emma-Jane & Tan
Eugenia Kim
Express Design Studio

F
Fenton Handbags
Ferragamo
Filson
Foley + Corinna
French Connection
Frye

G
Gap
Gara Danielle

Gerard Darel
Gigi Favela
Giuseppe Zanotti Design
Gorjana
Graham & Spencer
Gucci
Guy Baxter

H
Hat Attack
Hermès
Hudson Jeans

J
J Brand
J.Crew
Jack Gomme
Jean-Michel Cazabat
Jennifer Alfano
Jill Platner
Jil Sander
Jimmy Choo
Joseph
Jutta Neumann

K
Karen Karch
Karen Zambos
Kate Spade
Katherine Azarmi-Rose
Kristen Lee

L
L.A.M.B.
Lee Angel
Lenny
Levi's
Limited, The
Liz McClean
Loeffler Randall

Lolli by Reincarnation
Lulu Guinness
Lyell

M
Manolo Blahnik
Marc by Marc Jacobs
Marc Jacobs
Marni
Mason by Michelle Mason
Maud
Mayle
Michael Kors
Michael Stars
Minnetonka
MINT Jodi Arnold
Mischen
Missoni
Moschino Cheap & Chic

N
Nanette Lepore
Natalia Brilli
Nicole Farhi
Noir
Nolita

O
OK47
Opening Ceremony

P
Paige Premium Denim
3.1 Phillip Lim
Philosophy di Alberta Ferretti
Pierre Hardy
Plenty by Tracy Reese
Pomellato
Pono
Prada

R
R.J. Graziano
R&Y Augousti
Ralph Lauren
Ralph Lauren Blue Label
Ray-Ban
Rebecca & Drew
Renata Mann
Repetto
Réyes
Robert Normand
Robert Rose
Rosa Chá

S
Saja
Sergio Rossi
Seven For All Mankind
Shana Lee
Sisley Paris
Sondra Roberts
St. Kilda
Stella McCartney
Steven Alan
Streets Ahead
Swatch

T
Tara Subkoff for Easy Spirit
Tashkent by Cheyenne
Ted Rossi NYC
Temperley London
Tevrow + Chase
Thea Grant
threeASFOUR
Tiffany & Co.
Tory Burch
Trovata
Twinkle by Wenlan

U
United Bamboo

V
Valentino
Vanessa Bruno
Vena Cava
Vivienne Westwood
Vivienne Westwood Anglomania

W
Walter
Wayne Lee
WD-NY
What Comes Around Goes Around
Wyeth by Todd Magill

Y
Ya-Ya
Yigal Azrouël
Yves Saint Laurent

Z
Zac Posen
Zoe Chico
Ziji

photo credits

acknowledgments

Thanks: Roanne Adams, Jennifer Alfano, Maylis Atkins, Cori Bardo, Nissa Bothoff, Ann Brady, David E. Brown, Bridget Buckley, Liz Carey, Andrea Ceraso, Faye Chiu, Francis Coy, Daniel del Valle, Gaelle Drevet, Matthew Egan, Emma Fletcher, Jen Ford, Erika Forester, Claire Hansen, Annamarie Ho, Coco Joly, Rashida Jones, Jean Godfrey June, Jason Kass, Nancy King, Karyn Kloumann, Wayne Lee, Alexa Levitt, Lauren Marino, Monet Mazur, Jillian McAlley, Emily McCarthy, Liz McClean, Melissa McNamara, Dona Monroe, James Morris, Lauren Nathan, Richard Petrucci, Brianne Ramgosa, Alexandra Richards, Ji-Eun Rim, Meredith Rollins, Charlotte Ronson, Holly Rothman, Jessi Rymill, Jeffrey Schad, Susan Sheeran, Bill Shinker, Donna Sollecito, Regan Solmo, Mary Ta, Alex Tart, Shoshana Thaler, Anna Thorngate, Keisha Whitaker, Rebecca Wiener, Carl Williamson, Joan Wolkoff, Betty Wong, Megan Worman, Kate Wright, and Christine Zalocha.

This book was produced by Melcher Media, Inc.
124 W. 13th Street
New York, NY 10011
www.melcher.com

Publisher: Charles Melcher
Associate Publisher: Bonnie Eldon
Editor in Chief: Duncan Bock
Executive Editor: Lia Ronnen
Associate Editor: Lindsey Stanberry
Production Director: Kurt Andrews

Text by Charlotte Rudge
Store Guide by Elise Loehnen
Market Editor: Tiffany Pasqualone
Casting Director: Fiona Lennon
Photo Editor: Jaime Keiter
Lucky Breaks Editor: Liz Kiernan
Fashion Assistant: Jamie Barton

Design by Naomi Mizusaki, Supermarket

Cover Design by A/C

Gotham Books Published by Penguin Group (USA) Inc.375 Hudson Street, New York, New York 10014, U.S.A. Penguin Group (Canada), 90 Eglinton Avenue East, Suite 700, Toronto, Ontario M4P 2Y3, Canada (a division of Pearson Penguin Canada Inc.); Penguin Books Ltd, 80 Strand, London WC2R 0RL, England; Penguin Ireland, 25 St Stephen's Green, Dublin 2, Ireland (a division of Penguin Books Ltd); Penguin Group (Australia), 250 Camberwell Road, Camberwell, Victoria 3124, Australia (a division of Pearson Australia Group Pty Ltd); Penguin Books India Pvt Ltd, 11 Community Centre, Panchsheel Park, New Delhi - 110 017, India; Penguin Group (NZ), cnr Airborne and Rosedale Roads, Albany, Auckland 1310, New Zealand (a division of Pearson New Zealand Ltd); Penguin Books (South Africa) (Pty) Ltd, 24 Sturdee Avenue, Rosebank, Johannesburg 2196, South Africa

Published by Gotham Books, a member of Penguin Group (USA) Inc.

First printing, October 2008
10 9 8 7 6 5 4 3 2 1

Gotham Books and the skyscraper logo are trademarks of Penguin Group (USA) Inc.

ISBN 978-1-592-40402-5

Printed in China